D0849531

*Ending*

*Wars*

*Well*

# ENDING WARS WELL

*Order, Justice, and Conciliation in
Contemporary Post-Conflict*

Eric D. Patterson

Yale UNIVERSITY PRESS

*New Haven & London*

Copyright © 2012 by Eric D. Patterson.

All rights reserved.

This book may not be reproduced, in whole or in part, including illustrations, in any form (beyond that copying permitted by Sections 107 and 108 of the U.S. Copyright Law and except by reviewers for the public press), without written permission from the publishers.

Yale University Press books may be purchased in quantity for educational, business, or promotional use. For information, please e-mail sales.press@yale.edu (U.S. office) or sales@yaleup.co.uk (U.K. office).

Set in Minion type by IDS Infotech, Ltd.
Printed in the United States of America.

*Library of Congress Cataloging-in-Publication Data*

Patterson, Eric, 1971–
   Ending wars well : order, justice, and conciliation in contemporary
post-conflict / Eric D. Patterson.
      p. cm.
   Includes bibliographical references and index.

   ISBN 978-0-300-17113-6 (cloth : alk. paper)   1. Peace-building—Methodology.
   2. Peace-building—Moral and ethical aspects.   3. Postwar reconstruction.
   4. Just war doctrine.   5. Reconciliation.   I. Title.
   JZ5538.P3732 2012
   327.1'72—dc23

                         2011046033

A catalogue record for this book is available from the British Library.

This paper meets the requirements of ANSI/NISO Z39.48-1992 (Permanence of Paper).

10 9 8 7 6 5 4 3 2 1

*For those who serve our nation*

# Contents

# Preface

One of the conundrums of the scholarly community is the way that different disciplines and methodological approaches can exist in separate silos, without ever communicating with one another in a meaningful fashion. This book seeks to address at least two such divides. The first is the chasm between the study of war and the study of peace. Advocates of the latter, particularly in "peace studies" and "conflict resolution," have a set of practices and formulas for peacebuilding, arbitration, and reconciliation. Scholars of the former—particularly when it comes to inter-state war—tend to focus on the causes of war, such as competition for natural resources, the role of aggressive individuals or oligarchs, the security dilemma and spiraling distrust, arms races, revanchist and revolutionary ideologies, trade wars, and the like. The gap between those who really understand the variability and complexity of war's causes and those who are deeply concerned with individual and collective conflict resolution tends to be gaping in terms of methods, concepts, and philosophy. A second disjuncture is between the world of policy, often informed by academic resources in political science and international relations theory, and the world of academic philosophy departments. The former, to which I am admittedly partial, is deeply concerned with marrying ethics with real-world practice in a timely fashion. The latter can provide valuable contributions, but much of the literature seems disengaged from the true responsibilities faced by public officials and the competing nature of "lesser evil" policy alternatives available to democratically elected leaders.

This book seeks to bridge some of these gaps. On the one hand, it is deeply rooted in just war thinking and it attempts to extend that thinking to late- and post-conflict. At the same time, it applies just war thinking to real-world cases where flesh-and-blood people make decisions about war, economics, security, and development, all the while in the environment of political flux. The book will be a success if its parsimonious framework of "Order-Justice-Conciliation" can be a guiding heuristic or mental schema for students, researchers, aid workers, diplomats, soldiers, and statesmen. In other words, what does Afghanistan (or Sri Lanka, Sudan, Colombia, the Balkans, or any other conflict-ridden society) need? Order first and foremost, perhaps some attempt at Justice, and over time, if practicable, policies of Conciliation. Order-Justice-Conciliation is the model for a robust but flexible approach to post-conflict policies that are both moral and pragmatic.

This book would not have been possible without the support of Bill Frucht and his team at Yale University Press and my colleagues at Georgetown University's Berkley Center for Religion, Peace, and World Affairs. I am particularly grateful to those who read chapters of the book, including Dan Philpott, Pauletta Otis, Charles Villa-Vincencio, and any others that I may have unintentionally omitted. I especially thank Robert Van der Waag for his comments on the entire manuscript, as well as those of two anonymous reviewers. The work was enormously assisted by my research assistants, primarily Ilan Cooper and Elizabeth Royall, but also Vanessa Francis, Caryl Tuma, Joseph Shamalta, and students from my post-conflict seminars. Finally, I am deeply appreciative of my wife, Mary, for her support of yet another writing project.

This book is dedicated to those who serve and support the United States abroad in conditions of conflict and post-conflict, particularly the armed forces, the diplomatic corps, and development experts.

## CHAPTER 1

# Ending Wars Well

The defining conflict of our time is the 2003 Iraq war. Iraq's multidimensionality of issues—preemption, prevention, sovereignty, terrorism, religion, the obligations of post-war reconstruction, the role of the UN, and the like—combined with the visceral, personal effect it has had on millions of people makes it more than a regional conflict or historical footnote. Iraq is the illustrative case of our generation, the war from which historians, academics, policymakers, and students will draw analogies, comparisons, and lessons for the foreseeable future. Many debates continue concerning the decision to use force, how the military instrument was employed, or the preparation for, and implementation of, post-conflict activities (what the military calls "Phase 4" operations and what the U.S. Department of State calls "reconstruction and stabilization ops").

Today we know a great deal about the strategic and operational assumptions made in planning for post-conflict Iraq. We know, for instance, that the U.S. military was prepared for a longer, harsher, bloodier "hot war" against the Iraqi military than actually occurred, and that it even was equipped for a war that would likely include biological and/or chemical weapons. Nonetheless, the senior leadership, such as Defense Secretary Donald Rumsfeld, believed that the "use of force" would not last longer than five months. Expecting a liberation, not an occupation, Rumsfeld told reporters in November 2002, "I can't tell you if the use of force in Iraq today will last five days, five weeks or five months, but it won't last any longer than that."[1] This attitude shared a basic philosophy articulated a decade earlier by then-chairman of the Joint Chiefs of Staff, General Colin Powell, that the purpose of the U.S. military is to act on behalf of American interests: to "fight and win the nation's wars."[2] Battlefield victory culminating in regime change was the goal in Iraq.

The goal was met; Iraq's military and political apparatus crumbled in six weeks before a fifty-four-nation invasion led by the U.S. and Great Britain. However, both supporters and opponents of the war were horrified to see the chaos that followed the toppling of the Ba'athist regime, and many in America could not understand how those Iraqis who greeted Coalition troops as liberators in May 2003 were murdering their neighbors and blowing up Americans just a few weeks later. The next eighteen months were a time of ongoing sectarian violence, cunning insurgency, and opportunistic criminality claiming thousands of Iraqi lives. The "post-conflict" environment refused to improve, ultimately verging on a civil war in 2006 after (Sunni) terrorists affiliated with al Qaeda-in-Iraq blew up the golden-domed Samarra mosque, a historic and holy Shia site. As counter-terrorism expert David Kilcullen writes, it took four months for the U.S. military to realize what Iraqi politicians knew from day one: "that Samarra was a disaster that fundamentally and irrevocably altered the nature of the war."[3]

It is too simplistic to look back and say that the U.S.-led coalition failed to plan for the aftermath of the hot war. Tactical and operational planning did occur in the U.S. at both the Departments of State and Defense.[4] In fact, the planning resulted in some successes, such as preserving Iraq's oil infrastructure from the kind of destruction that followed the liberation of Kuwait in 1991. Nonetheless, the real failure was the lack of a strategic and moral framework for post-conflict, not just for Iraq, but also for places like Haiti, Kosovo, Afghanistan, and the Democratic Republic of Congo. This is not simply the failure of leaders in Washington, but also of those in London, Paris, Madrid, Berlin, Geneva, Turtle Bay, and elsewhere.

This book is not a critique of those failures, but it is a response to them. The argument that follows is that policymakers need a parsimonious framework—a way of thinking about—post-conflict obligations and priorities rooted in prudence and ethics. Such an approach should be simple enough to be applied on a case-by-case basis to a diversity of real-world scenarios, yet rich enough to provide a range of theoretical and practical answers to the difficult questions of post-conflict. And the questions are pressing: What is the moral nature of security? Can there be a just post-conflict, even if the war itself was unjust in some way? Do liberators have some obligation to provide a "just" occupation? How can we resolve tensions between national security and justice? Between justice and reconciliation?

## Why Wars Do Not End Well

Before proposing some answers to these questions, consider an essential fact of contemporary warfare: wars rarely end well. "Ending well" suggests that security is achieved and that the past, present, and future have been taken into account: What caused the war, and can these causes be ameliorated or redressed? How was the war fought? Are there legitimate claims for justice due to the conduct of the war? How will the settlement and its implementation create a just and durable peace?

A quick survey of contemporary warfare—Sudan, Rwanda, Kashmir, Colombia, Afghanistan, the Arab-Israeli conflict, and elsewhere—suggests that wars rarely end well. Rather, they grind on and on, often sputtering out in a short-term peace deal that one or both sides renege on after a short breather. How is it that the characteristic of modern warfare is that wars do not end well?

Thomas Hobbes, author of the seventeenth-century political treatise *Leviathan,* wrote about warfare and governance while his own country was racked by civil war and while Europe bled itself dry in the Thirty Years War. Hobbes well describes a fundamental dilemma of post-conflict: "For war consisteth not in battle only, or the act of fighting; but in a tract of time, wherein the will to contend by battle is sufficiently known: and therefore the notion of time, is to be considered in the nature of war; as it is in the nature of weather. For as the nature of foul weather lieth not in a shower or two of rain; but in an inclination thereto of many days together: so the nature of war, consisteth not in actual fighting; but in the known disposition thereto, during all the time there is no assurance to the contrary. All other time is peace."[5]

Hobbes was not arguing that states exist in a general condition of peace most of the time. Quite the opposite, his quip, "all other time is peace" is sarcastic, meaning that states in anarchy (no central authority) are always in a state of war, be it "hot" war or periods that we might today call pre- or post-conflict. In other words, at all times political units must expect a forecast of "rain" and must continually concern themselves with the vital matter of security.

When we look at the past half-century of European integration, the vital North Atlantic alliance, the peaceful demise of the Warsaw Pact and its former members' adoption of Western democratic capitalism, and the absence of major war west of the Danube since 1945, we might conclude that we live in a post-Hobbesian world, where the lessons of World War I and World War II resulted in new commitment to a just and durable peace. However, just a few miles beyond the Danube, Hobbes remains the prophet. Just east of the river is the still unstable scene of ethnic cleansing in the Balkans. Just south is

Cyprus, where a tense stalemate between Turks and Greeks continues unabated. Were one to trace a finger slightly south or east on the map, one would cover conflict-scarred regions that Hobbes, writing in 1611, would well have understood: Israel, the Palestinian territories, and Lebanon to the east; Sudan, Somalia, Rwanda, and the Congo further south.

The United States and its allies rightly congratulate themselves on achieving a stable post–World War II and post–Cold War consensus, but at the same time are flummoxed by the intractability of contemporary conflict. Why don't wars end well? Perhaps one would do better to ask, why should one expect them to—why is there a gap between expectations and post-conflict realities? There are a number of reasons that few wars have "ended well" since the fall of the Berlin Wall. Perhaps first and foremost is that the developing world has plenty of unfinished business to attend to, not unlike the violent clashes of the "new monarchies" and new states of Hobbes's day. Africa provides numerous cases in point, where European imperialists lumped disparate groups of people together within "national" borders, and/or favored one tribe over others, cementing hierarchy, inequality, and ultimately grievance. This is true of perpetually unstable Nigeria, created by the British and composed today of about 50 percent Muslims and 50 percent Christians representing hundreds of distinct cultural groups. The same is true of Sudan, which was historically two autonomous political units, but was merged under colonialism. Today countries like Sudan and Nigeria are wracked by political competition for scarce resources, exacerbated by differences of culture, language, religion, and ethnicity. In short, while Ottawa, Washington, and Oslo congratulate themselves on social welfare and the democratic peace, the people of Sudan and Nigeria are traumatized in the ongoing historical process of working out their internal contradictions, in much the same way that European states were in the sixteenth and seventeenth centuries.

A second thing that Americans seem not to notice is that many parts of the world have experienced conflict that burns on interminably. In contrast with our three years of involvement in World War II and one year of involvement in World War I—both entirely fought far from the continental U.S.—many Cold War–era proxy wars, such as those in Angola (1975–2002) and Afghanistan (1978–1996), were lived on a daily basis by their citizens over decades. Sudan has spent 40 of its 54 years since independence in civil war, and South Sudan's secession in July 2011 did not stop violence in Abeyi and Darfur. Colombia has spent most of the past sixty years in some form of civil conflict. Long-running wars slowly yet inexorably debilitate the possibility of a real security framework and peaceful coexistence among neighbors, such as in the aftermath of the decade-long Iran-Iraq feud. A related point is that many of the new wars since the fall of the Berlin Wall have been fought at home, by neighbors butchering one another. In contrast to American experience in the world wars, when "the Yanks are coming!" meant crossing an ocean to meet the enemy and then returning home shortly after V-E or V-J day, "going home" for most people in Nicaragua, Rwanda, or Mozambique meant living across the street from the perpetrator who raped and murdered their sister. And many of these wars, rooted in Cold War conflicts, were resourced by the ideological contexts and armaments of both the East and West.

Another reason that we lack a framework for ending wars well has to do with the myths of international relations. Such "myths" are organizing narratives that underlie international relations, which may or may not be true at all times and in all places, but that provide a conceptual orderliness to the consideration of international life. One of those myths is the idea that international relations is defined solely in terms of national governments ("states"), without other actors (for example, NGOs). Such a myth is characterized by state monopoly on the use of force within a given set of boundaries, and thus implies that a state should be free of intervention from its neighbors. This creates an unhelpful dichotomization between international and intra-state war. This fiction, however useful in the past, means that until recently attention was focused only on those conflicts that spilled out of their boundaries, thereby failing to notice massive depredations by governments and local warring actors against one another and their populace. It is true that since 1945 most conflicts have been civil wars, but a more nuanced analysis reveals that the wars/interventions the U.S. and its Western allies have participated in since 1945 were generally hybrid wars. The conflicts had definitive local sides egged on by outsiders, making them—like most wars in history—a hybrid of intra- and inter-national war. The same has largely been true since the end of the Cold War: many conflicts which have grabbed the attention of the West may have started as a "civil war" but were nonetheless clearly international in scope (the Balkans ultimately involved Russia, the U.S., the UN, and Western Europe; Rwanda destabilized, and plays power politics in, neighboring Congo; and Afghanistan is certainly such a hybrid). Whenever gross human rights violations result in international humanitarian intervention such as in the Balkans, Ivory Coast, Sierra Leone, Liberia, or elsewhere, the conflict is no longer a civil war but has rather taken on elements of an international conflict. Hence, we need a general framework for approaching post-conflict.

Another area where the West has a short memory is about the effectiveness of international intervention at comprehensively stopping the violence. Were one to look back before 1989 at instances of UN-led military interventions we would see that there were actually only two major cases: Korea in 1951 and the Congo in the 1960s. Both were large-scale, potent interventions involving tens of thousands of troops. These were the only cases of a major deployment of UN troops in wartime conditions, in contrast to puny "observer" missions like those in Cyprus and the Sinai. Indeed, when one looks at the UN Department of Peacekeeping Operations' list of operations, it is laughable—but not funny. Some of these impotent missions remain open, including: the UN Military Observer Group in India and Pakistan (1949–), the UN Peacekeeping force in Cyprus (1964–), the UN Disengagement Observer Force (Sinai, 1974–), the UN Interim Force in Lebanon (1978–), and the UN Mission for the Referendum in Western Sahara (1991–). The international community has decided nearly fifty times since the unraveling of the Cold War to deploy peacekeeping troops. Again, however, those deployments usually are small, have handicapping mandates (for example, Srebrenica), and lack punch to impose or ensure security for the local populace.

Since the end of the Cold War we have vastly expanded Western and UN involvement in late- and post-conflict, from Bosnia to East Timor to Iraq. The higher level of engagement in post-conflict situations has raised the awareness of citizens and leaders around the world that many people still live in a Hobbesian world. The level of violence compels us to do something, but we have not done a good job at ending these wars well. Perhaps we were unable to do so in the 1990s. That is what this book is about.

Furthermore, the West has been flabbergasted by the persistence of war because we cherish the idea that democracy and capitalism—in other words, human liberty—is the answer. This book is sympathetic to this view, and survey data report that the vast majority of people around the world want some culturally relevant form of political and economic freedom. That being said, this cannot happen all at once. Conflict zones do not become high-tech corridors overnight. What happens instead, in the aftermath of decolonization, conflict, or regime change, as described by Samuel Huntington in his 1968 book *Political Order in Changing Societies,* is that the thrill of decolonization or conflict termination evaporates quickly when Western political institutions, such as elections, parties, constitutions, and representative government, fail to rapidly deliver Western-level economic benefits.[6] This is a recipe for the unraveling of fragile new institutions and ruling coalitions, particularly because there are always spoilers and demagogues willing to leverage any uncertainty to their benefit. This was true in post-colonial states; it is likewise true at the end of most modern wars in the developing world. Moreover the success of the 1991 Persian Gulf War and liberation of Kuwait, coinciding with the end of the Cold War, blinded many to the fact that the war did not create a New World Order. Although Kuwait was liberated, the Gulf War resulted in a simmering sub-conflict that lasted for more than a decade, replete with a military confrontation, sanctions, scandals, and ultimately a second war twelve years later.

Globalization also plays a role in this current state of affairs, in at least two ways. First, it is common to say that globalization is "shrinking the world." As the world shrinks—via media (such as radio, movies, internet) and travel (tourism, services, and immigration)—the scope of our interest in world affairs has increased. For instance, just a few years ago vast domains of the world were simply inaccessible, largely due to the borders of the Cold War. In contrast, young people today think nothing of visiting places like Mozambique and Macedonia. The blend of native Western curiosity and wanderlust, in tandem with a much greater access to, and experience in, global affairs, provides a much broader stage for American compassion, as well as for American hubris. In other words, a shrunken world provides opportunities for observation of, compassionate concern for, and action in, grotesque conflict and post-conflict situations such as those in Aceh, East Timor, the Balkans, central Asia, and Africa. In short, we care more because we know more.

Yankee ingenuity and compassion also nourish American hubris, which is shared by many of our allies as well as the UN and multilateral organizations. That hubris is simply this: a desire to fix things. The West has tasted the bitter ravages of war in the past, but largely has avoided it for two generations and thus feels that it has lessons to share with other societies. Moreover, the technological prowess and wealth of the West provide it with a toolbox that can aid economic development and combat poverty. Nevertheless, there is a certain conceit mixed with the West's compassion, both because we rarely acknowledge the nexus of our ideals (improving human life) and our interests (access to raw materials) and because we fail to recognize that often what we think are the *seeds* of peace and security (access to water, sanitation, education) are actually the *fruits* of peace and security. In other words, our policy prescriptions and aid packages are rooted in Western standards of living and may overlook the brutal realities of order and security.[7]

The widening of our vistas for engagement in post-conflict, created by the Cold War's end and further nourished by optimism and ingenuity in a context of globalization, parallels a moral development in international affairs. That development is the evolution of notions of state sovereignty and human rights. On the one hand, the post–World War II era has seen the gradual rooting and growth of the doctrine of individual human rights, which is slowly changing the key referent for security from the state to the individual.[8] The Hobbesian bargain of individual allegiance to the state for perceived security, "no questions asked," has been stood on its head by those who argue that many citizens around the world have far more to fear from their own government than from neighboring countries.

The 1990s implosion of states (such as Somalia, Yugoslavia) and the domestic repressive behavior of other governments (for example, Sudan, Rwanda) called into question the Hobbesian bargain of allegiance-for-security, weakening the historic inviolability of state sovereignty in favor of protecting human life. The 1999 intervention in Kosovo, led by the U.S. without UN sanction, used this rationale.

The Clinton administration pointed to the Bosnian war just a few years earlier with its concentration camps, ethno-nationalism, and mass murder of civilians and said that Kosovo was becoming a similar violation of international law and human decency. Even without UN Security Council endorsement, NATO, led by the U.S., acted to halt the violence. However, as discussed in chapter three, this resulted in a long-term commitment to and massive investment in Kosovo's security. The Bush administration's exhortations for international action on Iraq, North Korea, Burma, Sudan, and Iran (and Obama in Libya) likewise used this rationale: morally abhorrent states lose the *carte blanche* of sovereignty—they are not legitimate authorities.[9]

Finally, the West, led by American power, won the three great wars of the twentieth century: World War I against old forms of imperialism; World War II against fascism; and the Cold War against Communism. We learned from World War I that post-conflict management was necessary because the unresolved issues or poor resolution of war's end will lead to the next conflict. The same mistake was not made in 1945; instead the West implemented political and economic programs designed to impose order and certainty in international affairs (for example, Bretton Woods, the UN, Marshall Plan, U.S. occupation of Germany and Japan). With the Soviet Union's collapse in 1991 the West again successfully reached out to many former adversaries, as evidenced by the inclusion of the former Warsaw Pact members in NATO and in the EU.

Of course, the question that remains is how this informs current conflicts and whether it applies to those places where we were not involved in the primary conflict in the first place. It is one thing to agree with General Colin Powell's two dicta: first, that going to war should be extremely rare, and, second, that "if you break it, then you will be responsible to fix it." But what if you were not the one who broke it? In some places, like lawless parts of Mexico and Colombia, the U.S. has clearly defined interests based on its commitment in the war on drugs. What about in Burundi? Kashmir? Sierra Leone? There are dozens of conflict and post-conflict settings around the world where the U.S. is not directly responsible and where many question whether to be (and how to be) directly involved.[10] The simple fact is, despite Powell's directive that U.S. involvement be limited, the U.S. and its allies tend to be more and more involved in late- and post-conflict situations. In a changing world, what is needed is not platitudes about reconciliation and a new world order, but a pragmatic approach, informed by our values, to address post-conflict environments based on those issues common to all, such as Order and Justice.

## Just War Theory and the Iraq War

In contrast to muddling through post-conflict issues whether in Iraq, Afghanistan, or elsewhere, Western governments have and utilize a strategic and moral framework for making decisions about how and when to use military force. That framework has evolved from the historically Christian just war tradition and has two basic components: under what conditions it is moral to go to war (*jus ad bellum*) and how violence can be employed and restrained during war in ways commensurate with just war values (*jus in bello*). Today, much of this framework is institutionalized in secular international law and the war convention. That convention originated with three criteria for the just decision (jus ad bellum) to use military force: *legitimate authority* acting on a *just cause* with *right intent.* Over time, additional factors were added to the original trio: *likelihood of success, proportionality of ends, last resort,* and *comparative justice.*[11] In addition, criteria were developed to inform and restrain how war is conducted (jus in bello): using means and tactics proportionate (proportionality) to battlefield objectives, which limit harm to civilians and other non-combatants (discrimination).

One can quickly see how this tradition, which goes back at least to Augustine in the fourth century A.D., undergirds international law; the common international principles of state sovereignty, the right to self-defense in international affairs, and the idea that governments are the only legitimate purveyors of military force all descend from just war theory. Similarly, the principles of proportionality and discrimination, often called "non-combatant immunity," are now part of Western military doctrine and the laws of armed conflict. Indeed, U.S. troops are refreshed annually on such principles, and these ideas have been enshrined in international covenants such as The Hague and Geneva Conventions, the Charter of the United Nations, and conventions on torture, genocide, and weaponry.

Just war principles inform policy choices and therefore were applied in many of the debates concerning both the decision to use force in Iraq and the conduct of the war—both for and against. Former U.S. president Jimmy Carter argued in the *New York Times*, "As a Christian and as a president ... I became thoroughly familiar with the principles of a just war, and it is clear that a substantially unilateral attack on Iraq does not meet these standards."[12] Just war theorist Michael Walzer concurred: "As opposed to the first Gulf War—a classic just war"—an intervention in Iraq would be "unjustified," being "against a distant and speculative threat which may or may not materialize," and leaving the United States "living with the dangerous consequences of military occupation."[13] Brookings Institution scholar William Galston argued, "The administration has repeatedly defined regime change not as the collateral benign effect of other efforts but as the end in view ... that formulation, at least, is outside the just war tradition."[14] Years later, President Obama's December 2009 Nobel lecture employed the language of just war: Iraq was not a "last resort" decision and thus was a war of choice, in contrast to the just war in Afghanistan.[15]

There were also just war arguments advanced in support of the war. Senator John McCain argued that the U.S. had a just cause and right intentions: "We fought a just war in Iraq to end the threat posed by a dictator with a record of aggression against his people and his neighbors and a proven willingness to use weapons of mass destruction against both."[16] Michael Novak argued that the war was a just closure of old business: "The reason why the United States is going to war against Saddam Hussein, unless he fulfills his solemn obligations to international order or leaves power, has nothing to do with any new theory of 'preventive war.' On the contrary, such a war comes under traditional just-war doctrine, for this war is a lawful conclusion to the just war fought and swiftly won in February, 1991."[17] Heritage Foundation scholar Joseph Loconte focused on the ethics of how the war was fought:

> In the end, [critics] argued that the fight to liberate Iraq is an unjust war waged with unjust means to accomplish ambiguous ends. Each of the anti-war predictions, however, has so far proven false. Indeed, it is difficult to recall any previous modern war being fought with such a sustained effort to protect civilians from combat and to minimize the harmful effects of war on their daily lives. This has come about because of intensive military planning, scrupulous attention to military targets, careful coordination among Coalition forces and unprecedented cooperation between the U.S. government, military and non-governmental relief organizations.[18]

What has been generally lacking in all of this debate, at least until very recently, however, is a similar moral and strategic framework for making planning decisions and ethical judgments about post-conflict.

Indeed, this is a persistent problem that the world community has failed to come to terms with in the twenty years since the

Cold War dissipated. There have been a myriad of small but deadly conflagrations around the globe, many of which the international community has responded to by sending peacekeepers. Indeed, in the first forty years of the UN's existence (up until 1989) there were only fifteen UN peacekeeping operations of any kind, but in the past twenty years, there have been forty-eight, over three times that number.[19] The conundrum of our time is that despite these efforts more wars keep igniting, old ones simmer along, and many countries revert to, or never get beyond in the first place, patterns of instability, insecurity, and violence. Iraq was not, as predicted, a five-month war; it has been an eight-year "low intensity conflict." Thousands more Iraqis will die in 2011; it is also quite possible that the killing will continue in 2012 and 2013. Many other parts of the world remain fragile, unstable, or contested. At any moment a new Bosnia or Rwanda could break out.

In sum, the past two decades have seen an increased willingness by the international community to send troops into harm's way, be it a modest peacekeeping effort or massive military intervention. But it is rare that a tidy post-conflict scenario of peace and security takes root quickly and cheaply. Part of the reason is the lack of a strategic, moral framework for post-conflict akin to existing just war thinking on the onset and duration of combat. New just war thinking can provide such answers.

## Just War Thinking on Post-Conflict: Jus Post Bellum

As noted previously, just war thinking is the basis for the laws of armed conflict and Western moral reflection on conflict, but it historically focused narrowly on ethical deliberation about the decision to go to war (jus ad bellum) and how war is fought (jus in bello). Chapter two sketches some of the historical and philosophical reasons that moral considerations of war's end (*jus post bellum*) have been neglected. Why do we need a prudential, ethically sound framework for ending wars well? It seems elementary: wars end best when they actually end. What is needed is an approach that moves beyond battlefield (and political) stasis to conflict termination. Jus post bellum should direct attention to resolving the fundamental causes of the war in question, including how the *cassus belli* may have evolved during the conflict; we seek a secure peace, not an intermission.

Jus post bellum should also attempt to balance the imperatives of security with considerations of justice. This is pragmatic in ending the costs of continuing warfare, but it is also moral in seeking justice that enhances security—such as the removal of warmongers like Slobodan Milošević from high office or restitution to victims. Efforts at justice can provide an opportunity in some instances for reconciliation. This is particularly important in civil wars: coming to terms with the past so that former belligerents can imagine a future lived together. In short, the application of a sturdy framework for ending wars well will have at its disposal a range of policy tactics such as security guarantees, reparations, and war trials, but will always have a clear focus on the tensions and potential of such policies with establishing security and political order.

This book employs a straightforward framework for ending wars well based on three concepts: Order, Justice, and Conciliation. As Figure 1 suggests, all wars should end with Order; Justice and Conciliation are important and valuable, but available in fewer cases.

Following a discussion of the just war tradition, its challengers, and its application to post-conflict in the next chapter, subsequent chapters are devoted to each of these three principles. Chapter three begins with the most difficult hurdle of all—simply getting to maintaining political order. Order in the form of security for all parties is a moral good, for it is impossible for domestic politics to provide the conditions of security necessary for what Greek philosophers called

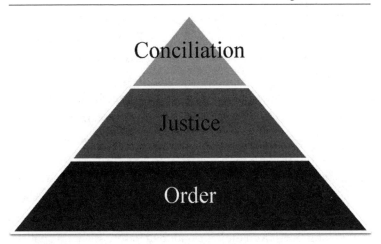

Figure 1: Elements of jus post bellum.

"the good life," meaning sufficiency within a rightly ordered society, without international security. Ending war in a way that rehabilitates or creates a political order is a monumental task. Chapter three explores the cases of Kosovo since the 1999 NATO intervention and Sudan's 2005 Comprehensive Peace Agreement to see how the principle of Order can be implemented and institutionalized in contemporary post-conflict.

Chapter four considers post-conflict Justice. Although such cases are few, particularly in the case of inter-state war, at times a richer dimension of jus post bellum has been employed that includes settlements with provisions for Justice. Justice means incurring what is deserved. In practice, Justice means holding aggressors accountable for their actions in some way. Justice may take the form of restitution, a payment of some sort to the aggrieved or the victim(s), or merely consist of a punishment of perpetrators. However, some efforts at restitution do not work well and, perversely, contribute to future violence, as in the case of World War I's Versailles Treaty. In order to understand these complexities chapter four examines mechanisms for justice in inter-state war (Iraq from 1991 to the present) and civil war (Rwanda). Chapter five is about Conciliation: coming to terms with the past. Conciliation is future-focused in that it sees former enemies as partners in a shared future. Sometimes, particularly in intra-state conflict, it is reconciliation—building bridges between parties that have some shared past. In international conflict, it is more likely that the goal is modest conciliation, the mutual effort of both sides to overcome past hostility and reframe the relationship as one of partnership. In either case, Conciliation is rooted in evolving collective interests, and it can expand and enhance Order and Justice under the right conditions. This chapter looks at a variety of models from the conciliation literature, including policies of amnesty, forgiveness, and reconciliation events, examining two cases: the 1979 Egypto-Israeli Peace Treaty and East Timor's multi-faceted national reconciliation campaign.

Over the past five years there have appeared a number of new articles from a variety of fields that talk about post-war justice, and, at times, even use the term jus post bellum. Much of the time, however, these other fields such as human rights law and conflict resolution operate from different assumptions than just war thinking. Chapter six explores the connections, and contradictions, between the just war tradition and these other post-conflict endeavors, such as the overlap between some transitional justice activities and jus post bellum justice, or the distinction between just war's emphasis on prudence and international law's rigid black-and-white approach to post-conflict justice.

The book concludes with a summation and a consideration of how a framework for ending wars well, rooted in the just war tradition, may evolve in the next decade to provide moral and policy guidance on planning for, and implementing, post-conflict activities in real world policy. The chapter looks at the contemporary challenges of Afghanistan as well as the growing set of government documents on "stabilization and reconstruction" (for example, Right to Protect, the U.S. Army Stabilization Manual) to consider whether these nation-building directives are congruent with just war theory's principle of restraint. In the end, the book calls on scholars and policymakers to flesh out this Order-Justice-Conciliation framework in order to end wars well.

## CHAPTER 2

# New Just War Thinking on Post-Conflict

In his Nobel Prize acceptance speech, President Obama became one of the few American presidents explicitly to acknowledge the just war tradition. Obama described the tradition's purpose as restraining or regulating the "destructive power" of violent conflict. Hence, according to the president, war is justified only if certain conditions are met, such as last resort and self-defense. President Obama also went on to describe the terror of unrestrained conflict, including holy wars and technologically sophisticated total wars. The just war portion of the speech reads:

> And over time, as codes of law sought to control violence within groups, so did philosophers and clerics and statesmen seek to regulate the destructive power of war. The concept of a "just war" emerged, suggesting that war is justified only when certain conditions were met: if it is waged as a last resort or in self-defense; if the force used is proportional; and if, whenever possible, civilians are spared from violence.
>
> Of course, we know that for most of history, this concept of "just war" was rarely observed. The capacity of human beings to think up new ways to kill one another proved inexhaustible, as did our capacity to exempt from mercy those who look different or pray to a different God. Wars between armies gave way to wars between nations—total wars in which the

distinction between combatant and civilian became blurred. In the span of 30 years, such carnage would twice engulf this continent. And while it's hard to conceive of a cause more just than the defeat of the Third Reich and the Axis powers, World War II was a conflict in which the total number of civilians who died exceeded the number of soldiers who perished.

In the wake of such destruction, and with the advent of the nuclear age, it became clear to victor and vanquished alike that the world needed institutions to prevent another world war.[1]

The speech recognizes the value of just war thinking for moral reflection on whether or not to go to war (jus ad bellum) and for ethical restraint on how war is fought (jus in bello), but it does not seem to apply whatsoever to the post-conflict phase.

President Obama is not alone in neglecting the application of just war thinking to war's end: traditional just war scholarship provided little formal theory on settlements, post-conflict justice, security arrangements, conciliation, and the like. Why did just war theory neglect jus post bellum? Are there alternative normative systems for ending wars well? This chapter provides answers to these questions and introduces some of the first flowerings of jus post bellum scholarship that have emerged in recent years—much of it spurred by the genocides of the 1990s and the wars in Afghanistan and Iraq following 9/11. To begin with, the chapter returns to other worldviews alluded to in President Obama's speech with contrasting ideas about how post-conflict should work, such as those of holy warriors who "exempt from mercy those who look different or pray to a different God."

## Moral Traditions in Conflict: Pacifism, Holy War, and Just War

In the Western tradition, there have been at least three ways to think about war: pacifism, holy war, and just war doctrine.[2] All three have strong roots in organized Christianity's first millennium, are in tension with one another, and have analogues in other religious, cultural, and secular traditions. For instance, Buddhism has internal cleavages between practical pacifism and the Buddhist warrior tradition (evidenced today in Sri Lanka); Islam has competing interpretations on the "lesser" versus the "greater" jihad and on the limits of restraint when fighting infidels; Hinduism has strong non-violent tendencies yet militant Hindu nationalism (*hindutva*) inspires conflict in Kashmir. Today, these religiously inspired traditions have secular siblings such as humanistic pacifism and ethno-nationalistic holy war, which share most of their essential assumptions and policy prescriptions.[3] Consequently, the three remain helpful frameworks for considering the normative content of warfare in the West, particularly in contrast to the just war tradition. Understanding how the philosophical assumptions of the pacifist and the holy warrior illuminates policy options for late- and post-conflict demonstrates the enduring value of just war thinking.

### HOLY WAR

President Obama's speech alluded to holy war when he described the "capacity to exempt from mercy those who look different or pray to a different God." Holy war is very different from just war thinking. The crusader believes that violence can be employed in defense of, or to further, eternal values. In practice, holy wars are often reactions to threats which seem to undermine the basic ideals and existence of one's civilization. Thus, the medieval Crusades and the Reconquista of the Iberian peninsula were perceived at the time as "holy" as they were repulsing the onslaught of heretical Islam in its religious and political forms. Contemporary proclamations to violent jihad in the Middle East are a response to perceived Western cultural and political domination.[4] Similarly, in the past century secular ideologies have provided moral justification for violence akin to "holy" war, such as Pol Pot's "Year Zero" agrarian Communism or kamikazes inspired by the *bushido* code.

What inspires the individual holy warrior? Skeptics like to note that material gain will stimulate the participation of some, as it did for many during Islam's early wars of conquest or the creation of Spain's empire in the New World. Nevertheless, many holy warriors are motivated by other concerns. For one, holy warriors are provoked to action by righteous indignation. Their most personal convictions have not only been questioned, but affronted and defiled. The crusader feels compelled to take action in defense of those ideals held most dear—faith in God and country. The holy warrior may also seek an eternal reward. This does not necessarily indicate a "death wish," but rather that the individual is convinced that his or her actions are in pursuit of transcendent ends and that such behavior will please the deity he or she worships. Of course, some holy warriors seek glory in both the here and the hereafter in the tradition of early martyrs of their faith.[5]

More could be said about holy warriors and jihadists, but the basic principle is clear. Holy war can be based on zealous love for one's faith, and such a love justifies employing violence. What concerns most critics of holy war is that, if the end is absolute—the defense of God's name—then it is difficult to provide any ethical rationale for limiting the means employed. As the Abbot of Citeaux famously told Simon de Montfort during the Albigensian crusade—before the slaughter at Béziers, France, in 1208—"Tuez-les tous; Dieu reconnaitra les siens" (Kill them all [including Christians], God will know his own).[6] Consequently, holy warriors are not content with a "settlement" because they are attempting to inaugurate God's kingdom on earth. Hence, the "excesses" of holy war: the extermination of entire cities during the rapid expansion of early Islam and the reactionary Christian Crusades, the Inquisition and wars of the

Counter-Reformation, the quasi-religious philosophy of the kamikaze, and the fatwas of Osama bin Laden resulting in al Qaeda's attacks on civilian populations. For the holy warrior, the transcendent end justifies any means.

What kind of post-conflict arrangement proceeds from the assumptions of holy war? If holy war is characterized by zealous love for one's faith, and often corresponding loathing for abominations that profane that faith, what kind of just peace follows conflict's end? First, for the holy warrior, war's end is a status of either victory or vanquishment: there is no intermediate state of affairs that can vindicate the end of conflict. Hence, negotiated settlements are simply not an option, excepting cases where they allow the weaker party a chance to fight another day. Assuming victory, the holy warrior must pacify or ameliorate the conditions that led to the moral grievance in the first place, often including a complete revision of the status quo. Such a "reformation" may include state-sponsored violence against "collaborators" with the old regime and/or it may include draconian enforcement of religiously informed codes of morality. This state of affairs is illustrated by the ambiguous concept of jihad. A debate raging among Muslim populations today concerns whether jihad is only an "internal struggle," such as mastery of one's vices in pursuit of personal holiness, or whether modern jihad should include the "lesser jihad": external struggle in society and on the battlefield. For the holy warrior, both views apply to the post-conflict space. The jihadist must win the battlefield victory over the forces of evil on behalf of his faith, but when that battle is over, a second battle begins—the struggle to overcome sin within the individual and eradicate it within the collective. Total victory goes far beyond the traditional battlefield. In short, the goal of holy war is not only to vindicate the faith, achieving spiritual glory as a consequence, but also to rightly order society along pure theological lines in the aftermath.

Historically speaking, the victory of Oliver Cromwell and the Roundheads in England's Civil War had many of these characteristics, including purges against Cavalier society and political elites and attempts to transform society, characterized by national laws (and corresponding prison sentences) covering everything from Sabbath worship practices to the colors of one's dress. More recently, we have seen how jihadists in Afghanistan (the Taliban) and Iran (since 1979) fight wars, including using human mine-sweepers, and also impose an unrestrained post-conflict "peace" within their realm. That "peace" is a totalitarian regime that punishes losers and promotes a doctrinaire code of political and social life that is idealized, intolerant, and brutish.

## PACIFISM

President Obama's Nobel Prize speech also referred to pacifism. Though citing the influence of Martin Luther King, Jr., and Mahatma Gandhi, Obama solemnized, "Make no mistake: evil does exist in the world. A non-violent movement could not have halted Hitler's armies. Negotiations cannot convince al Qaeda's leaders to lay down their arms." He went on to recognize the "deep ambivalence" that many countries feel about the resort to military force.[7]

Debates over pacifism in the West go back to the earliest years of Christianity and have a long tradition in some sectors of the Catholic Church as well as among Anabaptists, Quakers, Mennonites, and some other Protestants.[8] Many varieties of pacifism, including secular forms, are flourishing in mainstream Western society today, especially among European publics and American intelligentsia due to the legacies of the Vietnam War, nuclear weapons, and recent U.S. action in Iraq.[9] Contemporary pacifism (whether inspired by faith or not) is a commitment against violence and an allegiance to peace defined as nonviolence. In practice, Christian pacifists are motivated by Christ's commission to love one's neighbor, and secular pacifists often parallel this injunction with their own: "Do no harm." Moreover, Christian pacifists have looked back on Christ's example of self-abnegation and resignation to his fate as the archetype for their position. The pacifist faces war with two questions: 1) how could I, an agent of peace, be so presumptuous as to take someone else's life? and, 2) how could I be so vain as to employ violence in self-defense rather than accept God's design for my life? In short, the pacifist asserts personal responsibility for his or her own actions, and nothing more.[10]

This chapter is not a defense or critique of pacifism.[11] The question for our study of post-conflict is, "Can the pacifist position provide compelling normative and policy frameworks that public officials and soldiers can utilize for dealing with late- and post-conflict situations?" The answer is "not much." President Obama made this point in his speech: "But as a head of state sworn to protect and defend my nation, I cannot be guided by their [King, Gandhi] examples alone. I face the world as it is, and cannot stand idle in the face of threats to the American people. For make no mistake: evil does exist in the world . . . To say that force is sometimes necessary is not a call to cynicism—it is a recognition of history; the imperfections of man and the limits of reason."

Dozens of organizations and thousands of people inspired by pacifism work to change government policies (for example, through disarmament campaigns), serve as intermediaries between parties in conflict, and provide vital services amidst scenes of destruction and privation. However, the simple fact is that pacifism generally has provided a prophetic voice rather than useful policy prescriptions because of its fundamental commitment to peace in all situations. The pacifist vision for post-conflict is idealistic—peace without war—but it rejects the moral obligation of the state, as understood in international relations and just war theories, to be willing to utilize military force on behalf of a broader peace and security. Indeed, pacifism often seems divorced from reality, or suicidal, as state policy when contrasted with policies informed by Nazism, Communism, or violent Islamism. In the real world there are simply not examples of publics electing pacifists to the highest office of great powers or a track record of what a decidedly pacifistic foreign policy would look like under conditions of insecurity.[12] Pacifism, in theory or practice, does not provide a prudential, strategic framework for dealing with critical issues of national security and foreign policy in contemporary international affairs. In contrast, just war theory can and does.

### JUST WAR THEORY

Just war theory provides a middle ground between holy war and pacifism. The just war advocate agrees with the pacifist that war can be a costly, brutal endeavor and should be avoided. However, just war theory concurs with the holy warrior that there can be moral content to the decision to go to war (that is, to stop genocide), although disagreeing strongly with normative assumptions of holy war. As President Obama remarked in his Nobel Prize speech, "Our actions matter, and can bend history in the direction of justice."

It is this "bent toward justice" which suggests that just war approaches are actually a third vector, an independent focus, for contemplating the resort to force. The just war approach is based on issues of security, restraint, and justice rather than absolutism of any sort. It is the prudential nature of just war thinking that makes it useful to the policymaker because it applies not only to individual choices but to those of the states as well.

There are numerous statements of the traditional just war framework, including this reprinted from the United States Conference of Catholic Bishops.[13]

First, whether lethal force may be used is governed by the following criteria (jus ad bellum):

- *Just Cause:* force may be used only to correct a grave, public evil, that is, aggression or massive violation of the basic rights of whole populations;
- *Comparative Justice:* while there may be rights and wrongs on all sides of a conflict, to override the presumption against the use of force the injustice suffered by one party must significantly outweigh that suffered by the other;
- *Legitimate Authority:* only duly constituted public authorities may use deadly force or wage war;
- *Right Intention:* force may be used only in a truly just cause and solely for that purpose;
- *Probability of Success:* arms may not be used in a futile cause or in a case where disproportionate measures are required to achieve success;
- *Proportionality:* the overall destruction expected from the use of force must be outweighed by the good to be achieved;
- *Last Resort:* force may be used only after all peaceful alternatives have been seriously tried and exhausted.

Second, the just war tradition seeks also to curb the violence of war through restraint on armed combat between the contending parties by imposing the following moral standards (jus in bello) for the conduct of armed conflict:

- *Noncombatant Immunity:* civilians may not be the object of direct attack, and military personnel must take due care to avoid and minimize indirect harm to civilians;
- *Proportionality:* in the conduct of hostilities, efforts must be made to attain military objectives with no more force than is militarily necessary and to avoid disproportionate collateral damage to civilian life and property;
- *Right Intention:* even in the midst of conflict, the aim of political and mil itary leaders must be peace with justice, so that acts of vengeance and indiscriminate violence, whether by individuals, military units or governments, are forbidden.

It is beyond the scope of this work to catalog or comment on all of the strands of recent writing that have some connection to the just war tradition—but the language of the tradition remains rich, vibrant, and influential across disciplines. A half-dozen lines of contemporary inquiry are available to the interested reader. The first is the continuing relevance of both theoretical and applied jus ad bellum: are just war principles about the decision to go to war evolving? And, how should jus ad bellum be applied in the twenty-first-century context of rogue states, WMDs, and vicious non-state actors?[14] Part of this debate goes back to the attempt by quasi-pacifistic voices to reframe just war theory's traditional notion of the moral obligation of political authorities to "use the sword" with a "presumption against the use of force": an approach that continues to influence liberal Christian and secular voices in particular.[15] Perhaps the most interesting applied literature today is that which centers on the question of armed humanitarian intervention: how do sovereignty, non-intervention, and restraint stack up against the "just cause" of thwarting genocide and humanitarian catastrophe, such as in Bosnia or Rwanda or East Timor?[16]

A related literature continues to grow on issues of jus in bello: how should we think about the ethics of military tactics and operations, particularly as weapons evolve? What does the principle of proportionality say about nuclear weapons, weapons of mass effect, and non-lethal weapons used for crowd control?[17] What of distinctions between dictatorial political authorities in contrast to their conscript armies—who should be the proper locus of attack and punishment? Why is it legitimate to carpet bomb the conscripts but Saddam Hussein and Muammar Gadhafi are illegitimate targets? What about non-traditional actors such as "civilian" tribal networks providing logistical support to terrorists or insurgents and criminal cartels operating from hidden "sanctuary" within civilian centers?[18]

Three other areas of recent scholarship stand out. The first is comparative work on ethics and warfare in non-Western traditions, most notably diverse strands of thought in Islamic jurisprudence and history. There is clearly a discourse in the Muslim tradition about the morality of warfare such as proscriptions on denuding civilian agriculture, although Muslim traditions are multiple, distinct, and clearly not parallel to the Western just war tradition. Many of those intra-Muslim debates are still being worked out today, as a variety of voices claim moral legitimacy in deciding who can declare war, what the nature of "jihad" is, the range of justifications for employing violence, moral categories of combatancy and non-combatancy, and the like.[19] Second, there is a growing non-just war theory literature on the ethics of warfare. These approaches tend to be rooted in the human rights tradition or what Michael Walzer calls the "legalist paradigm,"[20] and use discursive moral reasoning to make rights-based claims about justice, political accountability, and rules-based decisions to employ force.[21] Finally, there is a collection of efforts to apply just war principles to non-traditional issues. Some of this work, such as that on sanctions and coercive diplomacy, is clearly within the tradition.[22] However, there are other publications that seem to conceptually stretch just war thinking beyond its logical limits, such as application to the environment and even the rights of animals.[23]

In sum, the just war tradition developed in the context of moral reflection on contemporary conflict: from Ambrose and Augustine watching Rome battle barbarians to Paul Ramsey's considerations of nuclear deterrence during the Cold War, Michael Walzer's *Just and Unjust Wars* written against the backdrop of Vietnam, and Jean Bethke Elshtain's evaluation of the first stages of the war on terrorism in Afghanistan.[24] However, despite its rich heritage and contemporary scholarship on jus ad bellum and jus in bello, this influential tradition has provided little sustained thinking on the ethics of post-conflict.

# The Just War Tradition's Historic Neglect of Jus Post Bellum

The question remains, however, as to why the venerable just war tradition has neglected jus post bellum considerations. As discussed later in this chapter, since 9/11 we have begun to see the first fruits of just war scholarship on post-conflict, but that does not explain two millennia of little more than platitudes, such as the oft-quoted "the end of war is a better state of peace." An examination of the possible reasons for these lacunae sheds light on several important issues, particularly the philosophical presuppositions upon which just war theory resides as well as changing views of war and war's end.

First, the fact that even today the majority of just war thinking concentrates on the ethics of deciding to go to war and how war is fought should not be completely surprising. From the Vandals battering at the gates of Augustine's beloved Hippo to the tit-for-tat between Predator drones and suicide bombers along the Durand Line, we have had century upon century of bloody, destructive warfare. Just war theorists have consequently focused their attention on the conditions and motivations of the conflicts at hand, analyzing their causes, the moral claims of antagonists, and the methods employed in combat. For instance, much of the first millennium of Western just war scholarship returned again and again to issues of pacifism ("Can one be a Christian and be in the army?") and holy war ("Is this Crusade justified?" "How should we respond to advancing Ottoman and Arab armies?"). Furthermore, as innovations in the nature, tools, and context of warfare have developed, just war thinking had to respond on a case-by-case basis, from siege warfare to obliteration bombing to nuclear weapons to remote-controlled aerial attack vehicles.

This relates to a point made in chapter one: many political theorists assumed, and continue to assume, that governments tend to be in a state of war rather than peace, either a "hot" ongoing conflict of actual combat, or a "cold" war of tension, strategic diplomacy, and commercial competition against known adversaries. As cited previously, Thomas Hobbes summarized this state of nature: "the nature of war, consisteth not in actual fighting; but in the known disposition thereto." This is the classic security dilemma. Ergo, debating jus ad bellum and jus in bello will remain important undertakings, particularly in today's uncertain era of state collapse, transnational terrorism, piracy, genocide, intra-state conflict, holy war, and preventive/preemptive warfare.

Nonetheless, there remain deeper, philosophical reasons that the just war tradition did not develop a formal framework for late- and post-conflict, beyond this practical reality that theorists were often preoccupied with war's initiation and methods. Perhaps the most important philosophical reason is that the tradition's earliest motivations were quite different from those which stimulate much contemporary just war writing. Today just war writing tends to focus on tactics; classical just war thinking focused on general principles. Political philosophers and theologians were focused on issues of justice and the rightly ordered society, and therefore the issues of morality and war were just one part of a much more ambitious and holistic intellectual project. For example, Augustine considered and defended the morality of Christians to serve in government, including law enforcement and the military, although there were strong anti-state (due to mandatory Emperor worship and public persecution) and pacifist tendencies among Christians. Yet this was only one small element of Augustine's larger project: the consideration of how legitimate authority in a fallen world could and should approximate the ideals of the City of God. Consequently Augustine, like the Greek and Roman philosophers before him, privileged political order (Pax Romana) over disorder (the Vandals who destroyed his home) as a moral good rooted in a wider theory about morality, justice, citizenship, legitimacy, and the state. According to Augustine, therefore, government officials had a moral obligation to buttress political order by preventing wrongdoing, righting wrongs, and punishing wrongdoers. This was true for both local criminals and predatory neighboring regimes.

Many of Augustine's intellectual descendants similarly located just war within a wider framework, the most famous example of whom is Thomas Aquinas. His master work, the *Summa Theologica,* is a massive compendium on theology, ethics, and what is today called political theory. However, he devotes only a couple of pages to just war in the entire treatise—despite living through the Crusades—because the focus is on a wider, comprehensive ethical system. The examples of Augustine and Aquinas remind scholars/theorists that just war thinking was a component of much wider systems of political ethics, and suggests that modern thinkers have largely lost this embeddedness of just war thinking within a larger normative system of politics and ethics.

Another reason that just war thinking neglected jus post bellum has to do with the tradition's fundamental purpose: restraint. Just war theory's purpose was never to provide a moral carte blanche for warfare (holy war), nor did it pretend that a non-violent world was possible or responsible (pacifism). Instead, just war theory's purpose was to call for responsible action while imposing limits, recognizing the moral obligation of leaders to defend and promote order, security, and justice in a fallen world. Indeed, the political ethic of responsibility inherent in the just war tradition expected, and continues to expect, that sovereigns (governments) rule their dominions with justice after the fighting has stopped. In other words, the just war tradition historically did not need a jus post bellum because there were robust religious, moral, and philosophical teachings—from the Old Testament to Aristotle to Aquinas—about the ethics of righteous governance. There was no need for a doctrine of jus post bellum when there was moral tradition, informed by chivalry, natural law, Christianity, and feudal obligation, governing how sovereigns were to act in peace.

Over the past five hundred years, there have developed at least two additional reasons that the just war tradition has not produced a framework for ending wars well. The Peace of Westphalia (1648) established the modern state system with its principles of sovereignty and non-intervention. Because war was defined as armed conflict between two sovereign powers, at conflict's end governments tended to maintain their sovereignty, with its accompanying principle of non-intervention, even if one had lost territory. In other words, in international politics it was nobody's business what the state did within its demarcated territory at war's end—even if that state was weak or despotic.

Finally, jus post bellum has been bypassed intellectually in the secularization and formalization of the tradition, the evolution of just war theory into what Michael Walzer calls the "legalist paradigm."[25] Over the past 100 years just war thinking has become a pillar of international law and the foundation of the war convention (for example, the Geneva Conventions), but as tends to happen in international law, the principles espoused become fixed and inflexible. Thinking largely stagnated for generations until well after World War II when individuals like Paul Ramsey and Michael Walzer breathed life into the tradition by examining tough moral cases in international affairs like global nuclear deterrence, the "supreme emergency" faced by adolescent Israel, and the tribulations of the Vietnam War.

Ironically, international law actually outpaced just war thinking in the area of post-conflict justice with the historic trials at Nuremberg and Tokyo and the establishment of the United Nations as a collective security organization to ward off threats to international peace and security. However, the promise of 1945 quickly froze with the Cold War and new problems—from atomic attack to counter-insurgency to genocide. In each case, the focus has returned attention to jus ad bellum and jus in bello, while the development of jus post bellum, either through moral statesmanship, philosophy, or international law, remained stunted. This book is an attempt to fill this intellectual gap.

## Recent Just War Thinking on War's End

Prior to the twenty-first century, there was virtually no just war scholarship on jus post bellum, but over the past several years this has been changing, albeit slowly. A look at the publication dates of this new literature demonstrates that just war thinking on war's end was stimulated by the events of the 1990s: Bosnia, Rwanda, Congo, Kashmir, Sri Lanka, East Timor, Sudan, Haiti, and Somalia. The conflagrations in Afghanistan and Iraq have added urgency to these considerations. Writing in this new sub-field within the just war tradition tends to focus on a discrete policy tool or controversy (for example, war crimes tribunals, obligations of occupiers), although a few authors call for post-conflict transformations that go beyond political rehabilitation to fundamentally change governing structures and relationships.

The wars in Afghanistan and Iraq have caused some authors to extend just war thinking to issues of Order in late- and post-conflict environments. Such writing tends to focus on the essential components of security: political order, the security of the populace, the nature of legitimate authority, just cause, restraint on the battlefield, proportionality, discrimination, and the like. For instance, Michael Walzer has advanced the idea of "just occupation": occupiers and the international community have a moral obligation to establish a stable, authentic, autonomous, and legitimate local government as soon as possible.[26] James Turner Johnson agrees, saying, "This means that for any use of force to be justified, it should not only respond to the disordering or absence of peace but should also include concrete plans for creating a peaceful society in the aftermath of conflict."[27] Gary Bass's research underscores the difficulty of reestablishing sovereignty in a post-conflict environment, such as organizing an autonomous legitimate government and local reconstruction.[28] Similarly, Robert Williams and Dan Caldwell suggest that a "just peace" is conditioned on restoring order, economic reconstruction, and reestablishing the political sovereignty of the defeated state.[29]

A second theme in recent writing on post-conflict is Justice. Doug McCready makes the case that a just peace will likely include punishment of aggressors and/or compensation to victims.[30] Davida Kellogg argues that war crimes tribunals, with their focus on punishing violations of the war convention, epitomize jus post bellum; tribunals are "in fact the natural, logical, and morally indispensable end stage of just war."[31]

There is a third point of view, beyond Order and Justice that advocates for Conciliation and more. This maximalist view tends to find arguments about security and punishment to be limiting, status quo, and conservative. The most important such author is Canadian philosopher Brian Orend, who posits seven tenets of jus post bellum, including the vindication of the rights of victims, full public disclosure of post-war aims and all settlements, principles of discrimination and proportionality informing post-conflict policies (for example, focus on leaders while protecting civilians), punishment, compensation, and "political rehabilitation." Orend's framework demands an expensive and expansive role for the victors—even if they were initial victims of aggression like Britain and the U.S. in World War II—including long-term financial and political guarantees ("reconstruction" and "rehabilitation") for the loser. Indeed, in an engaging presentation at Georgetown University in 2010, Orend argued for a new Geneva Convention for post-conflict that would mandate obligations on the international community with regards to post-conflict stabilization, reconstruction, and rehabilitation.

Others have likewise taken a maximalist stance, including Camilla Bosanquet, who calls for post-conflict demilitarization in the service of social restructuring,[32] or Louis Iasiello, who proffers a "healing mindset" and policies that "respect the environment."[33] Furthermore, as discussed in chapter six, there is a growing literature outside the just war tradition on amnesty, forgiveness, and reconciliation. British philosopher Mark Evans describes an "expansive" jus post bellum including "full and proactive . . . [action] in the ethical and socio-cultural processes of forgiveness and reconciliation, which are central to the construction of a just and stable peace."[34]

In conclusion, after nearly 2,000 years of just war thinking, it took the genocidal 1990s and the instability of Afghanistan and Iraq to begin to focus the attention of just war theorists on jus post bellum. As discussed in chapter seven, they were not the only ones late to the game—it was not until years after 9/11 that government agencies like the U.S. Departments of State and Defense began to issue guidelines for "post-conflict stabilization and reconstruction operations." This book consolidates and extends these principles of Order, Justice, and Conciliation, which I first wrote about in 2003, into a coherent framework for theorists and practitioners to apply in pursuit of ending wars well. It is to the foundation of that framework that this volume now turns—the challenge of establishing and maintaining Order.

## CHAPTER 3

# The Primacy of Order

On the evening of March 20, 2003 (Washington time), President George W. Bush approved a "decapitation" strike designed to eliminate Iraqi dictator Saddam Hussein, and perhaps avert, at the very last minute, a full-scale invasion of Iraq. The Iraqi regime had violated seventeen UN resolutions, and Coalition forces—led by the U.S.—demanded that Hussein leave the country and Iraq submit to weapons monitoring and verifiable inspections by the international community.

Hussein defied the UN, refused to depart, and the Coalition was ready to invade early on March 21 (Iraq time) when Bush ordered the decapitation bombing on two sites. Consider what might have happened if the strike had been successful: with Saddam out of the way and the Coalition marching in, the remaining Iraqi leadership might have sued for peace on terms that met the conditions of the international community yet kept Ba'athists in power. A revised regional political order would have ensued. Of course, in hindsight we know that the strike was unsuccessful, the Coalition attacked, and a military victory was achieved over Iraq's armed forces in approximately six weeks.[1]

However, conditions on the ground quickly deteriorated. Whereas jubilant crowds welcomed the Coalition as liberators in

March and April, a series of actions and inactions knocked the pillars out from under Iraqi society, causing widespread insecurity and the disintegration of the political order. Perhaps the first decisive blow to hopes for a new Iraq was the experience of ordinary Iraqis themselves—broadcast worldwide—as law and order dissolved: widespread looting, criminality, revenge killings, and lawlessness were ubiquitous. What shocked Iraqis, and CNN's viewers, were scenes of American troops passively watching the chaos without intervening.

To add fuel to the fire, Coalition Provisional Authority (CPA) czar Paul Bremer disbanded the already hollow Iraqi Army, dismantled several government agencies, and barred Ba'athist Party members from office. As party affiliation was necessary for almost any post under Hussein, including local police chiefs, doctors, and civil servants, this effectively destroyed formal governmental institutions, including law enforcement, the military, the judiciary, and the civilian bureaucracy.[2] Many of these individuals chose to support one of the many insurgent elements.

The Coalition won the war, but, at least in the short term, lost the peace. This is because a fundamental principle of politics was violated: the primacy of Order. Not only was the dictator deposed and his henchman eliminated, but Iraq's governing institutions were largely demolished, while the intervening forces allowed the country to burn. Preserving and promoting Order was a moral imperative as well as a pragmatic one for the Coalition, but they poorly discharged their duty in this regard. This reality—the fragility of political and social order combined with the moral and practical imperatives of leadership in post-conflict scenarios—is the theme of this chapter. Just war thinking provides a way to begin considering the priority and the quality of Order at war's end.

The first and most fundamental principle of jus post bellum is Order. All wars should end in ways that provide a minimal post-war order. The end of war should be a situation of stability and security, a modest goal that says little about justice, much less about reconciliation. Nevertheless, in the real world of bloody wars and dirty hands, a settlement that manages to provide for a post-war situation of security is a moral good.

Order begins with stopping the killing, which provides the political space for authorities to deepen the peace through basic security and essential services. More specifically, there are military, governance, and international security dimensions to a basic post-conflict order. The military (traditional security) dimension regards the definitive termination of "hot" conflict, with the tools of warfare resting solely in the hands of legitimate authorities. The governance (domestic politics) dimension is imposition and maintenance of the domestic rule of law, which requires a political entity to exercise sovereignty over its policies at home and abroad and focus on the fundamental tasks of governance, including the economic sector. The international security dimension means that the state no longer faces an imminent threat from an internal or external foe and that the country does not threaten the peace and security of its neighbors.

This chapter is a call to "slow down." In many contemporary cases, well-intentioned humanitarians, peace activists, human rights advocates, conflict resolution mediators, and transitional justice practitioners rush to pile on layer upon layer of their post-conflict stratagems prematurely—long before an adequate, durable security environment buttressed by modest but hardy institutions exists. Order has been taken for granted, or neglected, or eschewed as too primordial and atavistic in twenty-first-century models of peace and justice. But the reality is that before justice, conciliation, forgiveness, and all the socio-economic fruits of advanced democratic regimes can be addressed, the laborious work of thoroughly establishing Order as basic security and attendant political structures must be completed. This chapter begins with an overview from four important Western thinkers, from Aristotle to Huntington, of the necessity of Order and then sketches out the military, governance, and international security dimensions of such an Order. With this in mind, the bulk of the chapter then examines the triumphs and tribulations of recent post-conflict "settlements" in Kosovo and Sudan.

## The Elusive, and Fragile, Goal of Political Order

The previous chapter argued that just war thinking has its intellectual roots not in tactical thought about the strategy of war, but rather in a wider set of arguments about justice and the rightly ordered society. Just war thinking was and is the prudential application of that body of thought to the controversies of the day. A critical thesis from that literature is that political order in the form of security for all parties is a moral good, for it is impossible for domestic politics to provide the conditions necessary for "the good life" without a baseline of Order. The same is also true for international security. This notion is deeply rooted in Western political philosophy, and a full intellectual genealogy is beyond the parameters of this chapter. Therefore to introduce this intellectual heritage the chapter will limit itself to brief contributions from four thinkers on political order before fleshing out the description of post-conflict Order. What Aristotle, Augustine, Hobbes, and Huntington have in common is a simple thesis—political order is indispensable: humanity can be beastly outside the rule of law.[3]

Aristotle's (384–322 B.C.) writings on social and political life, notably his *Politics* and *Nicomachean Ethics*, argue that individual human beings cannot fully live "the good life" alone; they require the benefits of society in order for their needs to be met. Outside society a "state of nature" exists which is brutish and Darwinian. Human beings outside of society are "beasts": "Just as, when perfected, a human is the best of animals, so also when separated from law and justice, he is the worst of all."[4] This description could be applied to many post-conflict situations today. For Aristotle, it is only within society that law and justice, the foundations of political order and the bedrock of civilization, reign. Atomized individuals find it nearly impossible to provide for their basic material needs in nature, much less the aspirations and social comforts of civilization. Aristotle understood this first-hand: the Greek city-states had been at war for much of the previous century, first with the Persians and then among themselves. In this situation were one to leave the immediate protection of the city's walls, one was likely to be accosted by bandits or be caught in a crossfire of competing loyalties—a form of jungle law reigned. Aristotle, therefore, would not have been surprised by the insecurity of the Iraqi countryside or lawlessness beyond the city limits of Kabul; he knew that political order is the fundamental basis for any of the individual and collective goods humanity needs.

Augustine (354–430 A.D.) extended elements of Greco-Roman thinking on politics and society into the Middle Ages. Throughout his life he observed the retreat of Pax Romana with dismay; just before his death 80,000 Vandals invaded his home in North Africa and shortly thereafter Rome fell for the final time, issuing in the Dark Ages. Thus it is not surprising that political order is central to his magnum opus, *The City of God*. Augustine argued that society was rooted in a moral order, not simply the economic interactions of human beings.[5] Therefore, although human polities are poor reflections of the City of God, the political principle of temporal order approximates the eternal order and is worth defending.[6] To this end, authorities have a responsibility to Order and to Justice, including the use of the sword. Augustine adumbrated this obligation by quoting Romans 13:1–5:

> Let every soul be subject unto the higher powers. For there is no power but of God: the powers that be are ordained of God. Whosoever therefore resists the power,

resists the ordinance of God: and they that resist shall receive to themselves damnation. For rulers are not a terror to good works, but to evil. Wilt thou then not be afraid of the power? Do that which is good, and thou shalt have praise of the same. For he [the government official] is the minister of God to thee for good. But if thou do that which is evil, be afraid. For he beareth not the sword in vain: for he is the minister of God, a revenger to execute wrath upon him that doeth evil. Wherefore ye must needs be subject, not only for wrath, but also for conscience sake.

This conception of Order is not just preventing war or stopping the killing: it is a far wider-ranging moral project to reflect the values of justice and ethics found in the City of God. Political authorities have a moral obligation to prevent wrong and punish wrongdoing; such is testimony to a higher moral law and undergirds justice and security within the polity. Moreover, the destruction of political order means more than regime change—it is the destruction of civic order with all of its duties and opportunities for good living: medicine, science, arts, commerce, and the like. Consequently, Augustine would have clearly recognized today's threats of lawlessness and disorder—terrorism, piracy, insurgency—as striking at the very fabric of human morality and Order.

Thomas Hobbes (1588–1679 A.D.) proffered similar arguments about political order in his *Leviathan*. Hobbes was born a generation after Martin Luther ignited the Reformation in a Europe torn by religious and political strife. His adult life was lived in the shadow of Europe's deadliest war, the Thirty Years War (1618–1648), in which as much as a third of the German population perished. Similar to Aristotle, Hobbes famously described the fate of human beings outside a robust political order as "solitary, poor, nasty, brutish and short."[7] Hobbes makes a pragmatic argument for political order: individuals desperately need Order to overcome the natural state of affairs, which he defines as the "state of war." Self-interest demands individuals submit to some centralized order rather than kill one another in this state of war. Hobbes called that political order a "commonwealth": "The final cause ... in the introduction of that restraint upon themselves, in which we see them live in Commonwealths, is the foresight of their own preservation, and of a more contented life thereby; that is to say, of getting themselves out from that miserable condition of war which is necessarily consequent, as hath been shown, to the natural passions of men when there is no visible power to keep them in awe, and tie them by fear of punishment to the performance of their covenants."[8]

Hobbes's commonwealth is no utopia, but it is roughly secure—as evidenced by his naming it for the unconquerable mythical beast leviathan rather than after a more magnanimous creature (a Saint Bernard, for instance). It compels obedience and enforces a form of peace—the foundation, perhaps, for a richer security over time. In short, Hobbes would probably understand the war-weariness of populations in Afghanistan and Sudan and Somalia in the 1990s: people desperate to "get themselves out from that miserable condition of war" at almost any price.[9]

In the aftermath of World War II, dozens of countries achieved independence and/or transitioned to democratic rule, often as a consequence of civil conflict against their European colonial masters. In most cases Western-educated locals assumed the leadership of their countries with new democratic institutions enshrined in freshly printed constitutions modeled on that of the United States. But new constitutions, even when supported by millions of "aid" dollars, did not result in long-term politically stable, prosperous societies. Many crumbled into cyclic civil war and lawlessness.

In 1968 Samuel P. Huntington's *Political Order in Changing Societies* argued that the fundamental problem faced by these states was not poor constitutions, uncivil political cultures, or empty coffers. They suffered from a dearth of Order. What we might today call the

UN post-conflict menu—constitutions, elections, political parties, power-sharing—none of these substitute for centralized national power imposing a baseline of security. In fact, Huntington called existing development models "erroneous dogma" because they failed to see the irony of insecure post-colonial and post-conflict situations: changing societies have high expectations, but little patience, for peace, security, prosperity, participation, and better opportunity for their children. Mass mobilization and unrealistic expectations in the context of weak institutions is a recipe for disillusionment, despair, and demagoguery, leading towards dictatorship and/or war in fragile societies.

In short, the fundamental crisis that every country faces, whether just released from tyranny/imperial oppression or the crises of war, is establishing a durable political order. Although Huntington had post-colonial Africa and Asia chiefly in mind, his reflections apply to recent post-conflict environments like Bosnia, Afghanistan, and Burundi, where more is needed than paper constitutions and humanitarian assistance. What is needed is what Huntington, referencing Cicero (as Hobbes did before him), called a "commonwealth": a durable political order accepted by the populace. As long as political institutions are weak, ineffective, and plagued by corruption and as long as citizens do not feel safe, no such commonwealth is possible. In sum, security is the primal currency of political life; Order, even as just a modest security environment, is precious.

Aristotle, Augustine, Hobbes, and Huntington have provided only brief reminders of a perspective on war, peace, and society that undergirds the approach of this book: Order is the first principle. Without Order, Justice and Conciliation remain elusive. Of course, dozens more thinkers could be cited who emphasize this principle— as well as those who take an opposing view, such as those who put their faith in the brotherhood of mankind to produce a "perpetual peace" or the more contemporary perspective that post-conflict peace begins with forgiveness, human rights, and social justice. The chapters that follow will not neglect Justice and Conciliation in settlements, but will always do so against a backdrop of political order.

In post-conflict settings, what is political order? What does it look like? How can one work for it? In situations of late- and post-conflict, Order begins with stopping the killing. Order develops through the foundational element of security, meaning that the government can exercise sovereignty at its borders and within its borders, including a monopoly on the use of force at home. Order extends its roots through the maturation of government capacity and services. In practice, there are military (traditional security), governance (domestic politics), and international security conditions to a basic post-conflict Order that must be met and extended if there is to be lasting peace.

The military dimension regards the definitive termination of "hot" conflict, with the tools of warfare resting solely in the hands of legitimate authorities. This means that all belligerents have agreed to the cessation of conflict; there are no organized, armed spoilers or insurgents lurking in the countryside to destabilize the peace deal. Whether they were defeated or victorious, or negotiated a settlement, the leaders of all sides in the conflict support the new security arrangement by no longer challenging it via military force. The legitimate tools of warfare—usually in the form of small arms and light weapons, but also to include heavier armaments—have been reacquired by national or other (for example, peacekeepers) authorities, and often large numbers of military personnel drop their status as combatants and return to civilian life. Military considerations of Order also begin to take account of the appropriate structuring of military strength and forces to sustain a robust defense without undermining the security of formal rivals.

All of these efforts to confirm military aspects of a post-conflict Order should work in tandem with domestic and international political objectives while not undermining the fragile peace settlement. This last point is important because, ironically, it is possible that efforts in one sector can undermine efforts in another sector. A post-conflict settlement, for instance, that does not include all parties (as occurred for years in Burundi) or provides a military "solution" of demobilizing ex-combatants without a governance structure to absorb them back into civilian life, will undermine the Order, likely causing the resumption of violence and making future peace deals even more difficult to come by.

A second dimension of Order in post-conflict is governance (domestic politics). The governance dimension is imposition and maintenance of the domestic rule of law. It implies a national political entity that exercises sovereignty over the legitimate use of force as well as political sovereignty over its policies at home and in relations with its neighbors. However, in some cases the resumption of sovereignty has followed a period of political rehabilitation and tutelage, whether in the context of military defeat and occupation (post–World War II Germany) or political tutelage and reconstruction (Kosovo, East Timor). In either case, Order means focus on the fundamental tasks of governance, including over the economic sector.

Third, a basic political order has an international security dimension, which means that the state no longer faces an imminent threat from an internal or external foe. Likewise, the country is in no way a threat to the peace and security of its neighbors. The international security dimension is intertwined with and reinforces both basic internal security and efforts at governance. In sum, the very first steps toward a longer-term, more robust domestic and national situation of security begin with the arduous task of implementing political order in these three dimensions.

If we return to the opening scene of this chapter, Iraq following the end of major combat operations in April–May 2003, it is obvious that this principle of decisively establishing, or steadfastly protecting, political order was not implemented by the Coalition. Moreover, it was clear to al Qaeda-in-Iraq and other insurgent groups that the center of gravity was basic Order. Coalition forces were not prepared at the beginning, and with some good political reasons, to impose harsh conditions of military security (for example, martial law) that might look like an "occupation." But when CPA czar Paul Bremer dismantled Iraq's institutions and barred all Ba'ath party members from public service, he effectively emasculated indigenous military security and governance. More than eight years later, domestic Iraqi agencies still cannot keep the lights on, much less form effective governments pursuing policies of stability and justice. In terms of international security, although action against Saddam Hussein removed a real threat to his neighbors and an aggravation to the international community, the lack of Order—such as Iraq's porous borders or its vast unguarded arsenal—resulted in far-reaching, destabilizing influences across the region.

Just war thinking at war's end begins with efforts to rehabilitate or create a political order that is durable. Such Order, at the minimum, takes into account the modest yet difficult goals of domestic and international security. True, there are other grander, more inspirational visions of post-conflict halcyons. However, to end wars well the fundamentals must be firmly planted. Two recent cases provide a window into just how difficult and expensive the establishment of Order at war's end can be: the successful long-term international intervention in Kosovo, which began in 1999, and the faltering implementation of Sudan's Comprehensive Peace Agreement since 2005.

## Post-Conflict Order in Kosovo

Kosovo's 1999 conflict was an international, hybrid war—a case blending elements of historic ethno-nationalist antagonisms, insurgency, civil war, and outside intervention. It is an appropriate venue for considering Order, because the aspiration of the local citizenry was a revised political order and a primary objective of the international community was regional security. Furthermore, Kosovo's post-conflict order is a rare international case where the investment in Order is on par with the occupation and political tutelage that occurred in Germany and Japan at the end of World War II.

### THE KOSOVO WAR

In 1990 Slobodan Milošević revoked the historic autonomy that Kosovo and Vojvodina had enjoyed in Tito's Yugoslavia. The next five years saw a harsh subjugation of Kosovo that included replacement of all local security forces by Serbs, substitution of the Albanian-language school curriculum with a Serbian curriculum, and the replacement of most Kosovar government officials with Serbians. Albanian was eliminated as the official language of Kosovo and most of the faculty and students at Pristina University were fired or expelled. All Albanian-language newspapers, radio, and television stations were closed.[10]

In April 1996, coordinated attacks on Serbian security forces were conducted by a group calling itself the Kosovo Liberation Army (KLA). At first the KLA was small and poorly outfitted for battle, but this changed when the Albanian government collapsed in early 1997 during a financial crisis.[11] Armories and military supplies were looted with much of the equipment crossing into the border areas between Kosovo and Albania. This influx of weapons, along with money from Kosovar immigrants in Western Europe and the United States, allowed the KLA to rapidly expand. In March 1997 the Serbian government began sustained military operations against areas under the influence of the KLA while the KLA was attempting to control the border region with Albania to ensure a continued source of supplies and money from the outside world. The fighting continued the rest of the year and through much of 1998 with inconclusive results, but a downward trajectory. Serbian attacks in the fall of 1998 caused thousands of ethnic Albanians to flee their homes for the Albania border. With the winter coming, the Western allies feared a humanitarian crisis; there was also anxiety that refugees flooding into Albania and Macedonia would destabilize those countries. The international community feared a reprise of Bosnia's killing fields. U.S. Ambassadors Richard Holbrooke and Christopher Hill shuttled to Belgrade to convince the Serbians to sign a new peace agreement.

In January of 1999, Serbian paramilitaries razed the Kosovar village of Racak. NATO and the UN promptly declared the incident a massacre. NATO issued a statement declaring that it would use military force to compel compliance with the demands of the international community to reach a peaceful settlement to the conflict. With the Rambouillet (France) peace talks stumbling, NATO began a bombing campaign on March 24, 1999, that lasted for just over two months.[12] NATO told the media its goal was "Serbs out, peacekeepers in, refugees back."

The Serbs responded with concentrated ethnic cleansing operations that resulted in what was estimated as up to 1.5 million people being forcibly expelled from their homes (out of a population of less than 2 million). Thousands, perhaps well over ten thousand, were slaughtered. ICTY Chief Prosecutor Carla Del Ponte reported to the UN Security Council, in November 1999, that her office had reports of 529 killing sites and/or mass graves around Kosovo (an area the size of Connecticut). Hundreds of villages and towns were completely or partially destroyed; an unknown number of Kosovar women were systematically raped by Serb soldiers under the supervision of their commanders.[13]

The NATO air campaign was not initially successful, but ultimately the Serbs agreed to withdraw on June 12, as NATO and

Russian peacekeepers entered Kosovo simultaneously. Despite many setbacks, in the end a tenuous peace was implemented. The aerial campaign to win the war was about to transition to a decade-long experiment by NATO and the UN in creating and sustaining the post-conflict order.[14]

### KOSOVO'S POST-CONFLICT: EXPENSIVE, DURABLE ORDER

The Kosovo situation was déjà vu for international leaders: another Balkan crisis pitting Serbian *genocidaires* against impoverished Muslims. Many of the original cast of characters, most notably President Bill Clinton and President Slobodan Milošević of Serbia, were back on center stage. The hot conflict followed years of persecution, oppression, penury, and insecurity for Kosovars. In 1998 and early 1999 events seemed to careen down a well-trodden path: Serbian attacks and intransigence, Western diplomatic signaling, a mass exodus of refugees, the potential destabilization of the entire region, the disjuncture of Western and Russian interests, and ultimately a bombing campaign resulting in an end to the hot conflict.

However, international military action on Kosovo was unique in many ways, such as being a NATO-led (rather than traditional UN) intervention. More important, though, was the scale of the subsequent occupation. Kosovo differs from other peacekeeping examples by the sheer scale of investment and commitment by the international community. For years following the 1999 ceasefire, there were as many as 50,000 troops on the ground as part of the Kosovo Protection Force (KFOR) or the UN's companion UNMIK mission. Indeed, as of August 2011 there remain approximately 5,800 NATO troops on the ground in Kosovo protecting a population of just 1.9 million.[15] When these numbers are compared to other peacekeeping forces elsewhere, the differences are staggering. For example, the Democratic Republic of Congo lost 3 million people to war-related causes in the late 1990s but only has a UN force of about 20,600 peacekeepers for a population of nearly 60 million in a region equivalent to the southwestern United States.[16] East Timor, with half the population, received fewer than 8,000 peacekeepers at the height of the intervention there.[17] Perhaps most notably, at the end of the Bush presidency there were only 52,700 NATO troops in Afghanistan fighting a hot war in a country of 31 million people.[18]

More important than the numbers, however, is the quality of the peacekeepers. Most of us are aware that the preparedness, training, and equipment of peacekeepers from different countries vary widely. This was demonstrated most notoriously in Somalia, when some peacekeepers arrived on the scene without proper kits or weapons.[19] The recent UN/Africa Union mission in Darfur is a case in point as it has suffered from the weakness of its peacekeeping forces. Although recent UN budgets for Darfur are over $1 billion annually, for the first few years only one-third of the nearly 20,000 pledged peacekeepers showed up.[20] Moreover, many of those are from the world's poorest countries: Malawi, Burundi, Mali, Gambia, Burkina Faso, and Bangladesh.[21] The Kosovo case presents a direct contrast: the majority of the peacekeepers were Americans and Europeans, and they are among the world's most technologically sophisticated and finest troops.

It is clear that the long-term security commitment, which allowed Kosovo to achieve a large degree of internal stability over the past decade, is unique in international politics. Similarly, the investment by the West in Kosovo over the past nine years is equally startling. In 2009 alone, international humanitarian pledges to Kosovo were $1.6 billion.[22] To give a sense of perspective, international pledges for the UN Mission for the Ethiopian and Eritrean conflict for that year were less than 10 percent of those for Kosovo ($113 million).[23] In short, to date, Kosovo has had nearly a decade of significant financial investment in addition to imposed security that, ultimately, allowed this underdeveloped state to develop the infrastructure and institutions necessary for independence.

However, money and peacekeepers are not enough to make a viable country. Societies that thrive have governmental and non-governmental institutions that epitomize the rule of law and efficiently administer social services. Kosovo benefited from Western experts that significantly molded the development of Kosovar institutions and practices. Most notably in the final years before formal independence, former Finnish president Marti Ahtissari was designated UN envoy to Kosovo to report on its progress and recommend areas where it needed to grow prior to independence. The Ahtissari Plan, more formally known as the "Comprehensive Proposal for the Kosovo Status Settlement,"

> define[d] the provisions necessary for a future Kosovo that is viable, sustainable and stable. It includes detailed measures to ensure the promotion and protection of the rights of communities and their members, the effective decentralization of government, and the preservation and protection of cultural and religious heritage. In addition, the Settlement prescribes constitutional, economic and security provisions, all of which are aimed at contributing to the development of a multi-ethnic, democratic and prosperous Kosovo. An important element of the Settlement is the mandate provided for a future international civilian and military presence in Kosovo, to supervise implementation of the Settlement and assist the competent Kosovo authorities in ensuring peace and stability throughout Kosovo. The provisions of the Settlement will take precedence over all other legal provisions in Kosovo.[24]

The major points of the Ahtissari Plan, summarized below, sound like a playbook for jus post bellum. The Plan largely was funded, staffed, and implemented by experts from Europe and North America. Key elements of the plan included the following:

- Kosovo's security environment would be coordinated by NATO, a separate European Security and Defense Policy

Mission, and a special International Civilian Representative (from the EU). National military and police forces would be trained under these auspices.

- Kosovo's governance and legal institutions would be rehabilitated (or birthed in the case of a Constitutional Court) under the direct tutelage of outside actors. A new constitution, written under Western guidance, would promote multi-ethnic democracy, minority rights and participation, civil liberties, and human rights.

- Kosovo's economic development and humanitarian needs (for example, refugees) would be supported by the UN, other governments, NGOs, and others for an indefinite period of time.

- Cultural and human rights concerns would be safeguarded, from protective zones around dozens of places of worship to juridical proceedings against some gross human rights violations (again, under international tutelage).[25]

Of course, the Ahtissari Plan was couched in diplomatic jargon, but at the time everyone (including the threatened and angry Serbians) understood that the institutionalization of this document could lead at some point to the statehood of Kosovo.

For the past decade the UN has supported a wide assortment of institution-building and human capital projects in Kosovo: establishing a new justice system, operating a police force, coordinating the return of displaced persons, establishing a housing development agency, coordinating numerous economic stimulus programs, developing a national bank system, plus dozens of other developmental programs and agencies.[26] In 2007–2008 the United Nations budget for UNMIK was approximately $210 million.

Why did Kosovo receive all of this "tender love and care," particularly in contrast to other peacekeeping scenarios? Few in Western capitals in 1999 could have foreseen the incremental, short-term steps at military security, governance, and regional security that resulted in Kosovo's statehood. Nonetheless, it was clear during this decade that

Western leaders strongly believed in a Balkan domino theory: the violence in Kosovo could "spill over," most likely to neighboring Macedonia but also perhaps unravel the fragile Dayton Accord countries, most notably Bosnia-Herzegovina. Moreover, Serbian intervention in Kosovo might result in a broader war that introduced Albania—tied to many Kosovars by ethnicity, culture, and religion—to the conflict or, in a worst-case scenario, ultimately broaden into a larger civilizational conflict along Christian-Muslim lines that involved ex-mujahedin, al Qaeda fighters, or even Greece and Turkey.

Hence, the West was actively preventing another decade of Balkan disorder by decisive intervention in its neighborhood. It ultimately resulted in Kosovo's independence, which has been recognized by nearly seventy other governments and was affirmed by the International Court of Justice in July 2010. The West's interest in international security and its commitment to human rights overlapped in this case, resulting in herculean efforts to build a robust and enduring Order in this Balkan backwater.[27] In the end, this case of jus post bellum—decisive intervention, enforced security, massive financial support, and some modest efforts at justice and regional conciliation—is a remarkable case of imposed Order on a scale unseen since the occupation of Germany and Japan at the end of the Second World War. Perhaps the reality of its scale makes such an investment in Order sui generis, as the implementation of Sudan's Comprehensive Peace Agreement since 2005 suggests.

## Order Beyond Sudan's Second Civil War

Whereas Kosovo was a case of international war, Sudan provides an opportunity to observe the exigencies of contemporary civil war. Sudan has spent most of its life since independence in 1956 at war internally; it has the dubious honor of being one of the twentieth century's bloodiest battlegrounds. Hence, it is a tough case for implementing any form of post-conflict settlement. Yet in an innovative agreement affirmed by Sudan's neighbors and key outside actors like the U.S., the country entered a post-conflict "interim period" in 2005 that was followed by South Sudan's independence in 2011. This section looks at how Sudan's Comprehensive Peace Agreement (CPA) was intended to implement military and domestic security as well as rationalize government structures and institutions, and why the CPA does not seem to have the power to achieve a lasting political order.

### CIVIL WAR IN MODERN SUDAN

Modern Sudan was born in violence: months before Sudan formally gained independence from Britain in 1956 an armed uprising led by the southern-dominated Equatoria Corps resulted in seventeen years of secessionary struggle which concluded with the 1972 Addis Ababa Agreement. The issues of that first civil war remain largely the issues dividing northern and southern Sudan today: access to natural resources, the failure of Britain's (and Egypt's) plans to merge two historically distinct political and cultural units (the South and the North), and the cultural, ethnic, and religious differences between Arab-Muslim northern Sudan and sub-Saharan, Christian and animist southern Sudan. Tragically, it is estimated that a half-million people lost their lives in the conflict, with civilians accounting for 80 percent of the dead. Hundreds of thousands more lost their homes.

Sudan endured a fragile peace for about a decade (1972–1983), although internal political divisions (particularly in Khartoum between secularists, Marxists, and Islamists) kept the political atmosphere tense, unwieldy, and uncertain. However, in 1983 President Numayri announced his intention to implement sharia as state law. This was followed by a declaration of a state of emergency in April 1984. Numayri faced pressure not only from John Garang's newly formed (southern) Sudan People's Liberation Army (SPLA) but also from conservative Muslim clerics who questioned his legitimacy. The SPLA called for the establishment of an independent Southern Sudan, and continued its fight despite the ousting of Numayri and subsequent democratic elections in 1985. A contributing factor to the SPLA's suspicion of Khartoum during this period was that Numayri's "September Laws" implementing sharia remained on the books.

In 1989, Colonel Omar al-Bashir overthrew the government in a bloodless coup. Bashir continued the official policy of Islamization, including extreme punishments under sharia—for both Muslims and non-Muslims—such as amputation. Khartoum utilized religious propaganda to justify the state of affairs, recruit military personnel, legitimize Bashir's leadership, and reach out to various militant Islamist actors abroad, most notably providing a safe haven for Osama bin Laden and other "Afghan Arabs" for many years.[28] Khartoum also oversaw the development of a militia force, the Popular Defense Forces (al Difaa al Shaabi), distinct from the Sudanese Armed Forces (SAF), foreshadowing the type of internecine struggle that would later occur in both the south of the country and in Darfur. During the twenty-two years of this second civil war roughly 2 million civilians were killed and another four million displaced.[29] Such figures do not include the distinct conflict in Darfur.

### ENDING THE SECOND CIVIL WAR: THE CPA

Unlike in Kosovo, there was no armed intervention in Sudan. The civil war was brought to a close with what has become known as the Comprehensive Peace Agreement (CPA), signed on January 9, 2005. The CPA was negotiated between the Government of the Republic of Sudan and the Sudan People's Liberation Movement/Sudan People's Liberation Army (SPLM/A) over a two-year period (2002–2004), resulting in not one but six separate protocols with action addenda totaling well over 200 pages. The CPA process involved the Inter-Governmental Authority on Development (IGAD) composed of Sudan's neighbors (Kenya, Uganda, Egypt), and representatives from the Netherlands, Italy, Norway, the United Kingdom, the African Union, the United Nations, the Arab League, and the United States of America. These governments and agencies have provided services during the six-year "interim period" (following the CPA's signing) before 2011. UN Security Resolution 1574 (November 19, 2004) recognized the import of the CPA and called on all parties to aid its success.

Sudan's civil war ended with a series of six protocols signed over a period of more than two years. The Chapeau (preface) to the CPA records that "the conflict in the Sudan is the longest running conflict in Africa; that it has caused tragic loss of life, destroyed the infrastructure of the country, eroded its economic resources and caused suffering to the people of the Sudan" and that "peace, stability and development are aspirations shared by all people of the Sudan." According to the CPA, the negotiated settlement is based on "a democratic system of governance which, on the one hand, recognizes the right of the people of Southern Sudan to self-determination and seeks to make unity attractive during the Interim Period, while at the same time is founded on the values of justice, democracy, good governance, respect for fundamental rights and freedoms of the individual, mutual understanding and tolerance of diversity within the realities of the Sudan."

With these aspirations in mind, do the six protocols that comprise the CPA provide a structure for military security, governance, and international security? And what happened on the ground—did political order and security take root? Is continued "peace" likely, or should we anticipate a return to war?

The Machakos Protocol (July 20, 2002) established a six-year interim period [dated from July 9, 2005] during which the southern

Sudanese have the right to govern affairs in their region and participate equitably in the national government. The implementation of peace is to be conducted in ways that make the unity of Sudan attractive. After the interim period, southern Sudan had the right to vote in an internationally monitored referendum either to confirm Sudan's unity or vote for secession. With regards to religious law, sharia law is to remain applicable in the north, and parts of the constitution are to be rewritten so that sharia does not apply to any non-Muslims throughout Sudan.

The Agreement on Security Arrangements (September 25, 2003) specified a variety of military arrangements, including both an army of national unity composed of Northern and Southern troops as well as smaller forces loyal to Juba and Khartoum. Other militia and armed groups were to be disbanded, and the parties are to implement demobilization, disarmament, and reintegration (DDR) programs. Monitoring (not peace enforcement) was to be carried out by a UN mission to support implementation, as provided for under Chapter VI of the UN Charter.

The Agreement on Wealth Sharing (January 7, 2004) dealt with critical issues of access to land and oil revenues, splitting oil revenues evenly between the North and South (natural petroleum deposits are primarily in the South; Sudan's oil infrastructure pushes the oil to the North). North and South were to have parallel, but distinct, banking systems and currencies.

The Protocol on Power Sharing (May 26, 2004) provided for both a national government, with representation from both sides of the North-South conflict, and a separate Government of Southern Sudan (GoSS). For instance, the country has had two vice-presidents (one from the South) during the interim period, and there is proportional representation of northern and southern parties both in the national legislature and in state governments. A Government of National Unity was formed, though the federal government decentralized in many sectors, granting more power to individual states.

Finally, one of the most intractable sets of issues was addressed in the Protocol on the Resolution of Conflict in Southern Kordofan and Blue Nile States and separate Protocol on the Resolution of the Conflict in Abyei Area (both May 26, 2004). A variety of mechanisms were to be implemented to resolve boundary disputes, empower indigenous minorities, and allow for local referenda on the future of these states (Abyei is a contested, oil-rich area located on the North-South border).

## IMPLEMENTING THE CPA AS JUS POST BELLUM

The second Sudanese War lasted for twenty years and claimed the lives of nearly 2 million Sudanese, with another 4 million displaced. Hence, for war-weary segments of the population and neighbors affected by the conflict, the end of the hot phase of the war was a welcome development allowing people to return to, and rebuild, their homes, particularly in the southern parts of the country. Observers of, and advocates for, the CPA note additional strengths of the Agreement (on paper), most notably that it serves as an interim national constitution establishing the rule of law, thereby protecting the fundamental rights of citizens. This is a particularly important point when it comes to civil liberties (for example, freedoms of press, assembly), due process, religious freedom, and the issue of sharia, since one of the incendiary factors that started the conflict in 1983 was the implementation of sharia and Khartoum's notoriously restrictive approach to other liberties.

The CPA is designed to restructure a number of centers of power in Sudan. For example, it calls for the devolution of government functions in two major ways: first by providing a wide measure of autonomy and resources to the Government of Southern Sudan and second by elucidating mechanisms and resources for the empowerment of states. To this end, the CPA restructures the distribution of wealth both for short-term government revenues and for longer-term sustainable development. Most important, at least for the South, the CPA recognizes the reality of the Government of Southern Sudan's many parallel governance structures and legitimizes and resources them through wealth-sharing. The issue of revenue transfers was a key reason behind the collapse of the previous Addis Ababa Peace Agreement. The fact that the Government of Southern Sudan has been allocated 50 percent of net oil revenues generated from oil fields in Southern Sudan provides a key economic guarantee for effective implementation of the CPA. Moreover, the South had the option of autonomy and independence—which it took in the January 2011 popular referendum—at the end of the six-year interim period.

The CPA took pains to deal with what has become Africa's most difficult post-conflict problem: how to deal with oversized armies, ex-combatants, and the detritus of war. The Agreement created a new National Armed Forces consisting of the Sudan Armed Forces (SAF) and the Sudan People's Liberation Army (SPLA) as separate, regular, and non-partisan armed forces with a mission to defend constitutional order while providing disarmament, demobilization, and reintegration incentives to move the bulk of fighters back to civilian life. International support was provided for demining and ordnance clearance.

Finally, the CPA attempted to employ structures for effective monitoring of the elements of the agreement, such as the independent Assessment and Evaluation Commission charged with a midterm evaluation of the CPA's implementation. Furthermore, the CPA has a host of institutional and national witnesses and defenders who claim a commitment to the process: the Intergovernmental Authority on Development (IGAD), the African Union, the European Union, the League of Arab States, the UN, Kenya, Uganda, Italy, the Netherlands, the U.K., and the U.S.

Nonetheless, the CPA has encountered many roadblocks. First and foremost is the difficulty of implementing many of its key provisions. For example, many of the critical territorial issues remain unresolved following South Sudan's independence, and both sides have refused to stand down much of their (separate) armed forces. Violence is rising: North/South violence eclipsed the number of battle deaths in Darfur in 2009, and these continue to rise. All of this is exacerbated by the lack of robust outside intervention, or better security guarantees, on the ground. The UN force is a token observer mission, which has never demonstrated the mettle to head off a return to civil war. It does not even have a mandate to intervene to implement provisions of the CPA.

The CPA calls for the devolution of government functions in two major ways: first by providing a wide measure of autonomy and resources to a parallel Government of South Sudan (GoSS), and second by elucidating mechanisms and resources for the empowerment of states. To this end, the CPA was supposed to restructure the distribution of wealth both for short-term government revenues and for longer-term sustainable development. However, as reports from the International Crisis Group and the CPA Monitoring Group attest, even after five years the development of such institutions in destitute, war-ravaged South Sudan have made only the most modest of gains.[30] The South Sudan has a real government, including a robust public relations machine and mission in Washington, but it is weak like many other small, poorly resourced African governments. In part, this is because the CPA said little about how to transform the SPLM/A into an effective governing party rather than an army of national liberation. There is simply not enough indigenous human capital to fully realize modern mechanisms of governance in both Juba and the state capitals in the interim period (particularly in state capitals with little outside assistance and where there are major cleavages between the locals who are "sharing" power).

Long-term control of, or access to, the oil resources of South Sudan is a critical factor in the eyes of leaders in both Khartoum and Juba. Under the CPA, the GoSS was supposed to be allocated 50 percent of net oil revenues generated from oil fields in South Sudan, with the other half going to Khartoum. This provides a critical economic guarantee to the North. However, particularly in the South, the oil revenues have only improved the lot of a minority of citizens, largely around Juba; whereas in the North, oil wealth clearly is seen as an important prop of the Bashir regime, allowing it to continue to buy weapons and support SAF and *janjaweed* forces in Darfur. This was not the outcome intended by the international community.

International technical assistance to modernize financial and political infrastructure has been marginal, as most assistance to Sudan is humanitarian relief. For instance, the United States is the leading international donor to Sudan, providing on average $1 billion per year, but the majority of this goes to food aid and refugees, including those in the Darfur region. In FY 2010, for instance, 73 percent of U.S. assistance to Sudan was emergency food and other refugee/IDP aid with less than 10 percent going to political transition, governance, or security.[31] The CPA attempted to employ structures for effective monitoring of the elements of the agreement, such as the independent Assessment and Evaluation Commission charged with a mid-term evaluation of the CPA's implementation, not to mention pledges of support from various governments and regional associations, from the United States to IGAD to the Arab League. However, the National Congress Party, headed by Omar al-Bashir, has changed little over the past five years, and the combination of Southern dissatisfaction with the many outstanding CPA issues that remain unresolved (for example, Abyei) destabilize a tenuous situation. Despite the CPA calling for disarmament and a combined military for national unity, the CPA also allowed both sides to maintain separate (though smaller) armies in the field as well. Hence, for the South independence at the end of the six-year interim period through a popular referendum was eagerly anticipated in many quarters.

In addition, the censuses of 2008 and 2009 were corrupt, and the elections of spring 2010 were flawed. Just as the sharing of power, land, and wealth have been fractured and contentious, Sudan's national elections in May 2010 were roundly condemned by international observers as corrupt. For instance, the Carter Center declared, "Sudan's vote tabulation process was highly chaotic, non-transparent, and vulnerable to electoral manipulation."[32] Close observers of Sudan in 2009–2010 witnessed a return to levels of violence in some quarters typical of the civil war periods: the Council on Foreign Relations recently reported that in 2009 North-South violence eclipsed that in Darfur.[33] Whether independent South Sudan will ensure Order is yet unknown, but certainly the CPA processes have resulted in a more positive outcome than any dreamed possible a decade ago.

In sum, the close of Sudan's second civil war is quite different from the war in Kosovo. The Comprehensive Peace Agreement was a smart, thorough document with practical yet visionary aspirations for a unified Sudan. However, it is unclear that there was ever significant political will among some factions in both Juba and Khartoum to fully implement the Agreement. Moreover, the bullet points of the document are simply not enough to ensure a modest level of security, much less a society marked by justice, equality, individual freedoms, and national reconciliation. Those elements of the CPA dealing with long-term security and political order were hamstrung, poorly funded, and/or lacked tangible support from partnering countries—often due to the intransigence of Khartoum. The UN mission on the ground lacks the capacity and mandate that NATO forces in Kosovo have enjoyed, and outside of Juba proper, there has been little development of human capital and infrastructure that will buttress a long-term Order as occurred in Kosovo. What happens next will largely be determined by people there, on the ground, establishing or undermining domestic security, governance, and regional security.

## Conclusion

South Sudan and the Balkans remain uncertain, volatile places today, but they have both benefitted from the investment and interest of the international community. They are quite different cases, Kosovo an untraditional international war including military intervention by NATO and Russia; Sudan a classic civil war fought over decades. Nonetheless, as in Iraq, both cases demonstrate the difficulties of just stopping the killing to achieve an agreement on a basic framework for post-conflict peace. At the heart of such efforts must be guarantees and investment in practical security, which means not only human survival but taking the first steps toward a political order wherein citizens can pursue what Aristotle called the "good life"; outside that Order life is "nasty, solitary, brutish, and short." It is the disruption of this Order that has been the shared goal of Sudanese janjaweed and militias, Serbian paramilitaries, and insurgents practicing sectarian torture and gruesome executions in Iraq and elsewhere.

There are, at a minimum, military, governance, and international security dimensions to a basic post-conflict order. The military (traditional security) dimension regards the definitive termination of "hot" conflict, with the tools of warfare resting solely in the hands of legitimate authorities. In the case of Kosovo, powerful international actors have guaranteed security with boots on the ground while attempting to demobilize and demilitarize the populace. In contrast, Sudan's interim period under the CPA remained volatile as military integration and demobilization were thwarted by political uncertainty and rivalry. A governance (domestic politics) dimension is a necessary aspect of political order, as can be seen in the development of institutions in Kosovo. Sudan also has institutions, but they are parallel systems between Khartoum and Juba and likely foreshadow more conflict because there is little shared governance or national identity. Finally, all contemporary conflicts, even civil wars, have various international dimensions: Kosovo and Sudan threatened to destabilize their regions. We have seen that even a truce, ceasefire, or peace agreement is simply not enough to maintain long-term stability: there must be a commitment by all former belligerents to the revised political order.

Getting to war's end is difficult enough, but in some cases it is possible and desirable to move beyond Order to Justice. To that the book now turns.

## CHAPTER 4

# Justice
## *Incurring What Is Deserved*

Following the disastrous Russian winter of 1812–1813, Napoleon's disintegrating army staggered back to France. Despite the horrors of that winter, including hunger, cold, and partisan attacks, Napoleon and the French army survived to win several battlefield victories the next year. It was simply not enough; the coalition against Napoleon took Paris in March 1814. Napoleon determined to march on the city, but his generals—led by Ney—forced him to step down. Napoleon's abdication and the ostensible end of the Napoleonic Wars were written into two lenient treaties, those of Fontainebleau and Paris. In the former, Napoleon abdicated the French throne but retained his title of "emperor" and was made sovereign of the Mediterranean island of Elba. In the Treaty of Paris (signed May 30, 1814), post-revolutionary France was welcomed back to the European system, including a return to its antebellum January 1792 borders, reacquiring most of its lost territories.

This conciliatory "solution" was not enough. Within the year, Napoleon escaped Elba, regained the French throne, and threw Europe back into mayhem. This time, however, after being soundly defeated at Waterloo, he surrendered to a British navy captain, requesting political asylum. Napoleon cleverly surmised that he was most likely to be treated with *noblesse oblige* by his British foes but faced an altogether different reception should he fall into the hands of Prussia or Russia. Ultimately, a second Treaty of Paris (November 20, 1815) was signed, finally ending the Napoleonic Wars and setting up the "concert" system of European great power stability.

The 1815 Treaty of Paris imposed harsh terms on both the French leadership and the French people. Napoleon was held in confinement for some time and then exiled to bleak St. Helena in the south Atlantic under careful British supervision. Some of his marshals were murdered (Brune) or executed by firing squads (Ney, Berthier). France lost territory, was forced to pay indemnities of 700 million francs, and was saddled with the cost of supporting a 150,000-man army of occupation for up to five years.[1]

The two treaties of Paris had different notions of how to best end the quarter-century of upheaval since the explosion of the French Revolution in 1789. The first treaty (along with Fontainebleau) sought to reconcile France to the Concert of Europe system as a Great Power among Great Powers, with little cost for all of its warmaking. That system did not survive the year. The second treaty punished the leader, Napoleon, and punished France itself in ways that weakened its ability to make war. This system, which included punition prior to eventual conciliation, became the foundation for a half-century of peace between France and its neighbors.

Why it is that Justice, in the form of punishment, is often necessary to really bring a conflict to a close? What is the relationship of Justice to Order? What arrangements of Justice are most likely to evolve into stable political environments? What ethical architecture should punishment be founded on? What are the differences between policies focused on victims (reparations) and those focused on aggressors (punishment)? Between those focused on collectives and those focused on individuals? Finding answers to these questions is the subject of this chapter. Some wars can implement mechanisms of

Justice, consonant with political order, at war's end. This chapter looks at the application of Justice both in intra-state conflict, as in Rwanda, and in the aftermath of inter-state conflict (Iraq) to demonstrate how just war theory provides direction for pursuing Justice in some post-conflict settings.

## Just War Thinking on Justice at War's End

Justice presupposes that we live in a moral world where there is right and there is wrong. The historic just war tradition is rooted in Christian morality that defines good and evil, whereas secular just war thinking can point to international covenants and the laws of armed conflict—which nearly every government has committed to—as a shared morality in the society of states. This links to a concept from the previous chapter: the responsibility that governments have to sustain political order. The fundamental responsibility for governments is national and international security: this is the categorical imperative of states, the central ethic and fundamental duty of political actors. The flip-side of responsibility is accountability. In politics and war, governments—and the individuals who represent them—are morally accountable for their activities.

Simply put, Justice is incurring what one deserves. It is getting one's just deserts. In post-conflict settings this means that those who had responsibility for political and military choices that violated basic principles of humanity and/or the laws of armed conflict are accountable for their decisions and for their deeds. It also means that there should be some corresponding attention to the victims: what do they deserve?

As conceptualized in this chapter, Justice has a number of considerations. First, the pursuit of Justice—its implementation in law and policy—should not erode fragile post-conflict Order. It should not undermine the ability of belligerents to negotiate in good faith nor should it be so vengeful as to sow the seeds of future war. When framing peace settlements, ending the carnage sooner is often preferable to prolonging it in hopes of later "getting justice." Furthermore, in most cases post hoc juridical attempts to revise the original post-conflict deal, such as court cases against formerly amnestied military officers, are more likely to undermine the post-conflict social contract and heat up simmering tensions rather than help a society move on with the peace. The balance with Order must be maintained, although, in those cases where Justice will enrich and broaden the peace, it should be pursued.

Justice should reinforce the political order and the moral order. As Daniel Philpott writes, "justice involves practices through which the political order seeks to redress . . . those who have suffered" and "bring them to a state of greater human flourishing."[2] It is simply not the case that "anything goes in war." At a minimum the principles of just war, such as just cause and discrimination, in tandem with the tenets of the formal war convention and domestic laws provide a moral universe within which lawful, moral warfare can take place. Efforts at Justice, such as holding individual soldiers accountable for their misdeeds or political elites accountable for the orders that they gave, reinforce the moral order. They do so by reifying the rule of law, by "calling a spade a spade," by not pretending that there is some separate Darwinian law that makes armed conflict amoral. A host of other legal and moral violations often occurs during times of war, often perpetrated under the cover of the chaos, such as looting and rape by civilians taking advantage of disorder. So too, these injustices should be dealt with.

Justice can limit past wrongdoers. Conflicts that end with an austere post-conflict order are often unsatisfying because many of those responsible for injustice and violence retain their posts of authority with impunity. When it can be implemented, Justice moves beyond such a situation, demanding an accounting for transgressions and punishment for violators, confining perpetrators' future activities within strict limits (such as imprisonment or execution). This constrains wrongdoers from further violations, limiting the too-often cyclical nature of reprisals and resumption of conflict.

The issue of deterrence demonstrates the nexus of Order and Justice: robust justice activities should, in theory, deter future wrongdoing and therefore contribute to Order over the long run. However, justice-as-deterrence has a weak track record in international affairs, especially in contexts of weak institutions, fragile states, and especially stateless spaces like Yemen, Somalia, and parts of Colombia. For instance, it is hard to assess the deterrent possibilities of a targeted killing of a terrorist outside Mogadishu by a U.S. Predator drone—this is outright warfare and may be just punishment, but not deterrence. The same is true in international anarchy, at least until recently, where there are few cases of the political will in global affairs to act consistently against aggression in ways that would deter future wars. That being said, deterrence works for some crimes and restrains some criminals. The fear of getting caught, usually reinforced by strong preventive mechanisms, will deter some criminal activity. For instance, it is possible that the fear of punishment may restrain the behavior of combatants in battle (jus in bello); this is why Western governments routinely train their troops in the laws of armed conflict. Perhaps in the future a new track record of justice in international relations may help deter genocide and crimes against humanity in some contexts. Many had such high hopes a decade ago when they supported the establishment of an International Criminal Court. However, the Court's focus primarily on heinous crimes in Africa seems to have done nothing to deter, or restrain, the depredations of Robert Mugabe, Omar Bashir, Joseph Kony, and others.

Justice also provides something for victims. An element of Justice for some of those who were wronged is vengeance—the vindication of their righteous indignation, suffering, and loss. True, avenging the victims—particularly if some are already dead—does not necessarily solve all of war's problems, but it is a fundamental component of Justice and may be a critical element in longer-term healing of individuals and society. Justice means that aggressors pay some price for their misdeeds, and in some measure, there is a corresponding recompense to victims. In this sense Justice is restitutionary, although it is clear that monetary or other forms of reparations do not return to the grieving families their loved ones or their homes. Nonetheless, when some form of restitution that does not undermine the Order (such as draconian financial costs) can be implemented, it is a just mechanism for sustaining and enhancing the peace. Of course, we want that price to be discriminating (the right people paying) and proportionate (to the damage caused).[3]

Justice is the moral principle of incurring what one deserves. This is a modest, imperfect calculation in post-conflict situations and is often in tension with Order. Ironically, sweeping efforts at Justice can be imprudent or even destabilizing, but in those cases where some Justice is possible, it can help found and sustain a deeper, richer peace. The conception of Justice built on a foundation of Order that typifies this book is a modest, unhyphenated form of Justice, and consequently distinct from a growing body of adjectivized, elaborate forms of Justice including (re)distributive justice, restorative justice, transformative justice, or their progeny communal healing (as justice) and forgiveness (as justice).[4] To be specific, in practice, Justice at war's end proceeds from the principle of responsibility and generally takes two forms, restitution (to victims) and punishment (of aggressors). This chapter examines how these principles were implemented differently in the cases of Rwanda and Iraq.

## Restitution

Restitution means that victims or their representatives are entitled to recompense of something.[5] That something usually takes the form of a financial remittance that we call reparations. Reparations are at once an important symbolic acknowledgment that loss occurred, a compensatory act, and yet a weak approximation of the loss because it is often impossible to return what was taken or destroyed.

Restitution should not be conflated with punishment. Some mistakenly think that reparations are simply a "pound of flesh." This is not the case. Real restitution has to do with providing for victims and is separable from punishing wrongdoers. Indeed, restitution cuts across the conflict—it is possible that both sides "owe" something to victims of jus in bello violations, such as average citizens caught in Iraq's crossfires.[6] Although this issue is best considered on a case-by-case basis by studying the details of each situation, at a theoretical level reparations can provide an element of Justice to victims or their representatives in attempting to restore some of the conditions of the status quo ante bellum.

Restitution may take many forms, and the financial commitment may in fact be a "punishing" burden on a government, as Germany experienced at the end of the first World War when it had "accepted" war guilt, sacrificed (or restored) land to its neighbors, ceded its navy and much of its merchant marine to the victors, and paid reparations to the Allies.[7] This chapter will later look at the reparations model imposed on Iraq in 1991 by the international community, in which 30 percent of its petroleum sales were earmarked for reparations to Kuwaiti nationals and others.[8] In recent years, we have seen the U.S. military implement a local reparations system in the wake of collateral damage in military operations in Iraq and Afghanistan. In both theatres, military commanders have compensated victims and/or their families with "condolence payments" for non-combatant death, injury, and loss of property.[9]

As I have explained elsewhere, implementation of restitution raises many questions.[10] Should there be a statute of limitations on reparations, or should states (or victims) be able to sue for restitution for grievances that occurred in years past? A century, or centuries, past? In cases of regime change (such as post-Nazi Germany), does the new government owe something to victims on behalf of its predecessor? How does one disentangle, in post-conflict, the responsibility of governments (such as Iraq) from the policies of leaders (such as Saddam Hussein)? If the victims of aggression are long gone, is restitution to their descendants necessary? Does restitution contribute to international security? Beyond the questions of "to whom" and "from whom,"[11] how can a dollar value be put on the loss of life? Is a "condolence payment" simply hush money? How does one sift claims and counter-claims made by adversaries?

These questions highlight the practical dilemmas of trying to implement a reparations policy in the real world. However, reparations can be made to work, even in contradictory situations. For instance, in 2009 the Permanent Court of Arbitration at The Hague issued its final ruling on the competing claims of Ethiopia and Eritrea following their 1998–2000 war. The court ordered Ethiopia to pay Eritrea $163.5 million in compensation for destruction of Eritrean property and the imprisonment of Eritrean citizens and ordered Eritrea to pay Ethiopia $174 million in similar damages. In this case both sides accepted the verdict, with Eritrea paying Ethiopia a net of $10.5 million.[12] However, this is the rare case in international life—as the ongoing legal claims emanating from World War II or the World War I–era massacres often referred to as the "Armenian Genocide" demonstrate.

Finally, when it comes to the new wars of the twenty-first century—those perpetrated by non-state actors, terrorist organizations, and criminal cartels, reparations-as-justice seem fantastic. In sum, restitution can be a component of a holistic framework for Justice. Restitution may provide some damages to the victims but can never really repair or restore the ravages of war. In practice, reparations fall short of Justice because they are usually used as a substitute for punishment, and if used inappropriately can contribute to insecurity, as occurred in Europe in the 1920s and Iraq in the 1990s. Hence, policies of Justice should consider punishment of aggression whenever possible, particularly punishment of elites responsible for conflict.

## Punishment

Punishment is Justice applied to wrongdoers. It derives from the ethical responsibility that moral agents have in the decision to go to war and how war is fought. In application, punishment is the chastening and limitation of those who have done wrong; a penalty is imposed, usually the forfeiture of wealth, liberty, time, and perhaps even life. Whether it is loss of property, exile, incarceration, or execution, the principle remains the same—direct accountability for one's decisions and actions in warfare.

There are multiple ways to punish aggression in the aftermath of war. One is on the battlefield—to not merely compel one's opponent to sue for peace, but to ravage them before allowing the conflict to formally end—even though they are beaten. A second approach is to punish the citizenry itself in some fashion, such as forcing them into slavery or seizing land and property. A third approach is to punish the country through its institutions, such as by seizing military hardware, demanding government-to-government indemnity payments, or forcing official expressions of war guilt. Finally, punishment can be narrowly targeted at those responsible for aggression or war crimes, so that those with authority are held responsible for their deeds.

The idea that Justice has retributive features goes back to the earliest era of the just war tradition to Augustine, who argued that punishing those who provoke war is morally appropriate. In contrast, punition has come under fire in recent years, in part as a result of a larger agenda to limit the just war tradition to only narrowly defined, self-defensive actions. Oliver O'Donovan critiques the move as substituting "rights" for classical just war's emphasis on "justice," thus making the sole legitimate motivation for war self-defense of our own community's basic rights and thus any further war aims—deterrence, punishment, regime change, armed humanitarian intervention, or other revision of the insecure status quo—illegitimate. An ethic of self-defense of our collective's rights alone, rather than Justice more generally, absolves political authorities of any broader obligations to collective and international forms of security. In contrast, O'Donovan asserts that just war thinking includes the moral duties of governments to punish wrong, and he refers to Francisco de Vitoria, who criticized the Spanish conquest in the sixteenth century on just war grounds: "The victor must think of himself as a judge sitting in judgment between two commonwealths, one the injured party and the other the offender; he must not pass sentence as the prosecutor, but as the judge. He must give satisfaction to the injured, but as far as possible without causing the utter ruin of the guilty commonwealth."[13] Critics riposte with numerous questions about punishment as a moral principle and as policy. Is punishment just a "victor's justice"? How can individuals be tried for the crimes of states, and vice versa? Does the fact that only a small minority of violators is apprehended, and an even smaller number tried and convicted, call the entire claim of Justice into question? If war is hell, or at the least anarchy, are there really principles of Justice that can be enforced through punishment? Do not both sides have dirty hands at war's end? Should the international community avoid punishment because it leads to resentment . . . which leads in turn to renewed conflict?

These criticisms have been leveled at many trials, from Hermann Goering's claim that Nuremberg was a victor's justice to the more recent examples of Slobodan Milošević and Saddam Hussein deriding the illegitimacy of the legal mechanisms arrayed against them. However, the answers to these questions can be found in the discussion of Justice earlier in this chapter. First, regardless of the chaos of the battlefield, there remain moral principles and the war conventions under which government policies and the actions of soldiers should be judged. Moreover, even if punishment is imposed by a victor, that does not drain its moral content—it is still rooted in the moral principles of responsibility and accountability. Prudent punishment need not be the blunt instrument of World War I–style mass reparative payments; it can follow the just war criteria of discrimination (justice for the real perpetrators) and proportionality (justice proportionate to the misdeed), and therefore be less likely to result in disorder. Elite punishment, or punishment of a subsection of aggressors, is better than no justice at all, and its limits testify to the real-world boundaries of international life, and perhaps to the wise restraint of those who could seek more but choose not to. Punishment may or may not lead to resentment, but lack of justice may also lead to long-standing grievance and renewed conflict.

In conclusion, Justice is a foundational principle of the traditional just war paradigm, both in the decision to go to war and in moral culpability of actions taken during conflict. Justice is a critical principle of post-conflict as well, both as a theoretical principle and as a contributor to real resolution. Justice at war's end should, first and foremost, buttress political Order and result over time in increased security and stability. There can be real trade-offs or tension between fragile post-conflict Order and the desire for Justice, and judgment is called for in seeking Justice in ways that are complementary to Order. These tensions are apparent in the next sections of the chapter in dilemmas faced when implementing a program of justice in cases of inter-state conflict and civil war. In the former, Iraq following the two Gulf Wars (1991 and 2003), different modes of Justice are contrasted, first that of a victims-based, restitution model and later the elite punishment model that resulted in the execution of Saddam Hussein. In the second case, post-war Rwanda, the government deliberately chose policies of security and justice without reconciliation for the first five years following the genocide. As a shattered society, Rwanda faced many challenges in embedding Order and seeking post-conflict Justice, both in domestic courts and in the parallel UN-authorized International Criminal Tribunal for Rwanda.

## Punishment and Saddam Hussein

Saddam Hussein led Iraq as president for nearly a quarter century (1979–2003), having served previously as a senior Ba'athist official and one of the army officers that brought the Ba'athists to power in a 1968 coup. Hussein modeled himself on Joseph Stalin, so it should not be surprising that his reign was notorious for heavy-handed dealings against his own population, including torture, extra-judicial killing, and the use of chemical weapons on Kurdish villages, as well as attacks on neighboring countries (Iran, Israel, and Kuwait). The international community, led by the U.S., intervened in Iraq twice and imposed very different models of justice in each case: reparations in 1991 and elite punishment in 2003. The implementation of these models at the end of inter-state conflict demonstrates the challenges faced by a reparations-based model and tensions between Order and Justice.

### PUNISHING THE HUSSEIN REGIME—THE FIRST IRAQ WAR (1991)

Iraq invaded Kuwait on August 2, 1990, intent on quickly absorbing the tiny emirate into a greater Iraq, and thus acquiring its significant oil reserves. Saddam Hussein's regime pillaged the country, raping and killing those in their way and ultimately destroyed billions of dollars of government and private property, especially in Kuwait's lifeline—the oil sector. Over a million Kuwaitis fled the Iraqi army.[14] The ensuing savagery was nothing new; it followed the pattern of Iraq's grisly war with neighboring Iran through the 1980s. After months of negotiations and international threats, a U.S.-led invasion force under UN sanction invaded Kuwait and Iraq, liberating the former. With limited war aims, neither the George H. W. Bush administration nor the international community forced the issue: Iraq kept its pre-war boundaries and there was no march on Baghdad to depose the Hussein regime.

It is worth noting that at the time, there was considerable debate about how best to handle Iraq. What is often forgotten in retrospect is the international milieu of the time—the last gasps of the Cold War, the final year of the Soviet Union's existence, and the regional insecurities caused by fundamentalist Iran, vulnerable Saudi oil fields, and the simmering Arab-Israeli conflict—which made it a time of tremendous uncertainty and thus a certain conservative caution in Washington and at the UN.

Consequently the UN Security Council decided that the appropriate way to deal with Iraq was to force reparations on Baghdad to compensate its victims. UN Security Council Resolution 687 instituted such a mechanism: "Iraq . . . is liable under international law for any direct loss, damage, including environmental damage and the depletion of natural resources, or injury to foreign Governments, nationals and corporations, as a result of Iraq's unlawful invasion and occupation of Kuwait."[15]

A UN Compensation Commission was set up to determine claims and manage a fund for payment of war reparations. The Commission set up multiple categories of claims, including claims for individuals who had to depart from Kuwait or Iraq due to the invasion; individual claims for injury or death of a family member;

individual claims for loss of property or business; the losses of corporations, private sector enterprises and real property; and claims to be filed by governments and international organizations as well as damage to the environment.

The UN Compensation Commission reviewed claims, ultimately requiring Iraq to pay $53 billion. Only about a quarter of this amount went to individual claims (all of which were paid); the rest went to corporate and government losses. As of summer 2010, the government of Kuwait was still seeking $22.3 billion in reparations from the government of Iraq.[16]

As we consider the complex way that Iraqi reparations were paid in the 1990s, it is important to remember that there were at least two sides to the equation. The first, and most important, is that the Hussein regime was a predatory aggressor state that gobbled up its neighbor until pushed back by the international community. Iraq was directly responsible for at least $53 billion in costs, damages, and indemnities—but these massive amounts of currency say little about the pain and suffering of individual people, whether it be the loss of flesh-and-blood Coalition troops on mission to liberate Kuwait or the civilians of Kuwait. Incidentally, the survivors of the latter group—individual Kuwaitis killed—received only a modest payment of $2,500 for individuals and up to $10,000 per family.

Payments to ameliorate some financial and personal loss to Kuwaitis were one side of the reparations equation, as was compensation to international entities like petroleum companies and foreign governments who suffered loss due to Iraqi depredations. The other side of the reparations equation was the origin and process of payments made by the Iraqi government itself.

Ultimately the Iraqi government was assessed $53 billion. The process of generating revenue to pay the reparations was unique and novel. Iraq was already under duress from punitive economic sanctions instituted in 1990 upon the initial invasion of Kuwait. The UN

Security Council agreed to allow Iraq to sell a set amount of oil to meet its basic needs; 30 percent of Iraqi oil revenues went to a UN Compensation fund (25 percent after 2000) under UN Security Council Resolution 705 (August 1991). In 1995, the Security Council passed a follow-on resolution (UNSCR 986) which became the notorious Oil-for-Food Program. The Oil-for-Food Program was designed to channel profits above and beyond the 30 percent set aside for reparations specifically to humanitarian needs in Iraq, rather than have those funds go to modernizing Saddam Hussein's military or to supporting his lavish lifestyle. According to the UN, $31 billion worth of humanitarian supplies were available to Iraq under the program from March 1997 through November 2003, when the program was terminated and its vestiges absorbed by the Coalition Provisional Authority.[17]

By the time the 2003 Iraq war began, this reparations model was under some international censure. The program was criticized for the massive corruption that eventually was uncovered, which implicated even the son of the sitting UN Secretary General, and also for being too onerous on the Iraqi people. The latter criticism resonated around the world—that the program's indirect result was punishing average citizens with shortages of vital food and medicines while the Hussein regime continued living in sultanistic opulence. According to the CIA, Iraq's GDP dropped and remained through the 1990s a full third lower than its 1989 level.[18] A careful look at Iraq's finances by the Council on Foreign Relations in 2003 showed that the country was carrying $130 billion in foreign debt.[19] Thus the individuals truly responsible for invading Kuwait and overseeing the violations of the war convention—Saddam Hussein and his henchman—were virtually untouched by the reparations imposed in 1990–1991. Iraq was punished with economic sanctions, a war that decimated large elements of its military, no-fly zones, and political pariah status, but all of these punitive actions hurt the average Iraqi, not

Saddam Hussein. Indeed, Saddam continued to build palaces while millions of his people were receiving their daily bread from Oil-for-Food rations.

Was Justice done in 1991? A political wrong was righted in the liberation of Kuwait. Attempts were also made to prevent future wrongdoing by forcing the regime to accept a weapons monitoring program and limiting some of its freedom of action (as with no-fly zones). Most significantly, the international community imposed reparations on Baghdad. Virtually all of the individual and family reparations to Kuwaitis were paid, and much of the corporate and government losses were likewise paid. The rights of these individuals were vindicated by the legal judgment of Iraqi guilt, though the personal losses could never be fully recompensed by the modest cash settlement. On the Iraq side, much of the Kurdish and Shiite population experienced poverty and want in the Oil-for-Food era. The country was weakened, but the regime remained defiant and disruptive, ignoring UN resolutions and giving quarter to terrorists for the next decade. Members of the Ba'athist hierarchy and their minority Sunni base felt less of the hardships endured by their countrymen; in fact, elites prospered during the 1990s. In a sense, reparations were a benefit to Kuwaiti and some corporate victims, but the mistake of the international community was to conflate restitution with punishment, and think that reparations would constrain Saddam Hussein. Ultimately, the locus of "punishment" was simply not sufficient to restrain him.

### PUNISHING LEADERS IN THE SECOND IRAQ WAR (2003)

Following the U.S.-led invasion in 2003, Saddam's Ba'athist regime was dismantled, a Coalition Provisional Authority and subsequent interim Iraqi government assumed power, and Hussein himself went into hiding. For seven months Hussein eluded his pursuers, and he was ultimately captured by U.S. forces in December 2003.

In 2003–2005, representatives of the Iraqi people and the Coalition attempted to reconstruct Iraq's post-invasion institutions, despite spiraling insecurity and political flux. As described in chapter three, CPA Administrator Paul Bremer unilaterally disbanded the Ba'athist state and military. This "punishment" of the regime purged the government of all Ba'athist loyalists, but had the effect of destabilizing the country and pushing much of the educated workforce, including doctors, teachers, and lawyers, out of gainful employment and into the confidence of insurgent elements. This was an unwitting, but decisive, blow to post-conflict Order.

While the political and governance situation was evolving, a juridical process was set in motion to try Saddam Hussein and a few senior associates for genocide, war crimes, and crimes against humanity. The authority for the trial originally emanated from UN Security Council Resolution 1483 of May 22, 2003, which recognized the "authorities, responsibilities, and obligations under applicable international law" of the United States and United Kingdom as "occupying powers under unified command."[20] The U.S. and U.K. had already set up a Coalition Provisional Authority to administer Iraq which lasted until a transfer of power to an interim Iraqi government on June 28, 2004. Three days later, Saddam Hussein was arraigned in an Iraqi court before Iraqi judges. A year later Hussein and his co-defendants were charged specifically with crimes against the people of al-Dujail; the trial began on October 19, 2005.

Originally, the CPA had set up an Iraqi Special Tribunal (IST) under Order Number 48 to provide a judicial mechanism for trying senior members of the Hussein regime. By the time of Hussein's October 2005 trial, the Iraqi government had passed Iraqi Law Number 10 (2005), disbanding the IST and establishing the Supreme Iraqi Criminal Tribunal (SICT). The law sets out the rights of the accused, procedures for judicial tribunals, the appellate process, and the like.

According to the law library of the U.S. Congress, the proceedings were "a notable experiment in international jurisprudence [because] it is probably the first time a member state of the United Nations has chosen, without the participation or involvement of the United Nations, to bring one of its former leaders before a national court to try him for crimes recognized under international law."[21] Nonetheless, the SICT was based on both previous domestic and contemporary international law. The specific crimes to be addressed were limited, and those violations were taken from Iraqi Law Number 7 (1958), Iraqi Criminal Code Number 111 (1969), and the crimes of genocide, crimes against humanity, and war crimes. The penalties were to be taken from those enumerated in Iraqi Criminal Code Number 111. Interestingly, the description of genocide, crimes against humanity, and war crimes was taken directly from the Rome Statute of the International Criminal Court, which specifies that it is appropriate for future tribunals to observe the judicial precedents of penalties in courts such as the International Criminal Tribunals for Rwanda and the Former Yugoslavia. Like the tribunals for Rwanda and the former Yugoslavia, the SICT had chronological limits on its mandate (the period of Ba'athist rule from July 17, 1968, to May 1, 2003).

Ultimately, Hussein (and some co-defendants) sat through two trials. The first was for crimes against humanity (the crackdown on residents of Dujail following a failed assassination attempt) and the second trial was for genocide (the military campaign, including poison gas, against Kurds in Anfal). Hussein was found guilty on November 5, 2006, and his appeal was rejected. He was executed by hanging on December 30, 2006. Some of his co-defendants were likewise executed, some imprisoned, and others acquitted.

In sum, the aftermath of the 2003 Iraq war resulted in a different form of justice from the 1990s reparations model: elite punishment. The entire Ba'athist regime lost its privileged place in society, although by the end of 2004 the CPA reversed itself and began to allow low-level members of the party, usually desperately needed white collar professionals, to compete for government jobs.

The real focus of the Coalition, however, was on punishing Saddam Hussein and his senior auxiliaries. Rather than punishing the Iraqi citizenry through war guilt and war debt, a modern, juridical process in the vein of Nuremberg and explicitly following the models in Rwanda and Yugoslavia was implemented. Its direct outcome was the trials of Saddam and senior leaders in his regime; some were punished and others acquitted. The punishment model did not simply provide an avenue of justice for international aggression, but vindicated the suffering of many ordinary Iraqis as well. The proceedings dealt with previously unfinished business of local and regional aggression, helping to establish a new Order in Iraq and its neighborhood. Justice, in this case the execution of Saddam Hussein, was punishment directed at the perpetrator for causing conflict and for violations of the war convention, and thus was narrow, targeted, and ethically sound.

## Multiple Tracks of Justice in Rwanda

### THE RWANDAN GENOCIDE

The countries that we today know as Rwanda and Burundi have experienced ethnic conflict for decades, or perhaps for centuries. Following the end of Belgian colonial rule in the early 1960s and subsequent rise of the Hutu majority over the previously dominant Tutsi minority, ethnic violence occurred sporadically, including massacres by both sides. In 1990, under pressure from the international community, Rwandan president Juvenal Habyarimana allowed for the consideration of a multi-party democracy. However, fighting continued, and it was not until 1993 that the Tutsi-led Rwandan Patriotic Front (RPF)[22] and Habyarimana's

Hutu-dominated regime signed a peace accord. As part of the peace document, the Arusha Accords, about 2,500 UN troops (United Nations Assistance Mission in Rwanda—UNAMIR) were placed in Kigali to supervise the security of the capital and guarantee peace. All the while, Hutu paramilitaries and militias trained for an expected future confrontation.[23]

On April 6, 1994, the presidents of Rwanda and Burundi, Habyarimana and Cyprien Ntarymaria, were killed when Habyarimana's plane was shot down by a shoulder-launched missile. What occurred in Rwanda previously had been civil war; the killings that began within one hour of the plane crash were a premeditated, carefully planned Final Solution.[24] Roadblocks were set up by the Hutu-led Rwandan military and militias (*interahamwe*), and a radical radio station called on the Hutu majority to eradicate the Tutsi minority. Tutsis were systematically killed as forces went door to door seeking their prey. Within the first day, thousands of people were slaughtered, a number that grew steadily for the next twelve weeks.

The international community largely fled; most of the UN troops were recalled until General Romeo Dallaire only had 270 soldiers under his command.[25] Shortly thereafter the Tutsi-dominated RPF invaded Rwanda from its cantonment sites on the border, and in a dramatic push across the country, secured Kigali and swept the genocidaires toward the border with Congo. On June 22 the Security Council allowed French troops (Operation Turquoise) to enter Rwanda and create a safety zone, which protected many Hutu militants from the vengeance of the Tutsi-RPF.[26] The French handed off to an expanded UNAMIR force in August. In the end, an estimated 800,000 Tutsis and politically moderate Hutus were killed in a period of 100 days.[27]

The Tutsi-dominated RPF went on to form a government, establish a robust security environment and many functioning institutions and, within a decade, under the leadership of Paul Kagame (first as defense minister, later as president), was considered something of an African miracle. It held its first local elections in 1999 and its first real presidential elections in 2003. But what has most interested observers is not simply how the battlefield victory of the RPF initiated an end to violent conflict, but how Rwandan institutions—both formal and informal—as well as the international community have come to grips with the issue of Justice in this traumatized country. Rwanda is the rare case where real efforts at Justice have been made, both as a conscious step to enhancing the modest security occasioned by victory and as distinct and separate from any form of national reconciliation. Rwanda has made use of multiple tracks for justice, from traditional juridical processes to its famous *gacaca* courts to a unique UN-sponsored war crimes trial for elite decision-makers.

## THE EVOLUTION OF DOMESTIC JUSTICE IN RWANDA

In retrospect, the distinct but overlapping systems of justice that occurred in the Rwanda case can make a simple summary difficult. There are at least four phases in the evolution of justice in the fifteen-year period between 1994 and the present; our focus is primarily on the first decade of efforts at implementing justice. The first phase was simply the battlefield punishment that occurred against the perpetrators during the hot phase of the conflict—many were killed in battle or exiled either to French-protected camps or across the border into what is today the Democratic Republic of Congo (formerly Zaire). In such cases, the lives and property of many perpetrators were forfeit. Second, the post-genocide government of Rwanda incarcerated well over a hundred thousand alleged perpetrators, and attempted to deal with them for much of the next decade through its shattered criminal justice system. Simultaneously, in 1994 the UN

Security Council authorized an International Criminal Tribunal for crimes against humanity in Rwanda that sputters on to this day. For the first several years following the genocide, the policy of the Rwandan government was officially against forms of "reconciliation" that fell short of full Justice. However, a decade later Kigali fully implemented its famous gacaca court system to increase the pace of justice, decrease the volatile situation in overcrowded prisons and its weak traditional justice system, and ultimately begin a process of reconciliation at the local level.

In the summer of 1994 the emerging government of the RPF formally asked the president of the UN Security Council to begin a process whereby an international court would be set up in Rwanda to bring Justice following the genocide. The new Rwandan leadership clearly recognized that the country was decimated and that its mechanisms for law enforcement and criminal prosecution were reeling. However, when the Security Council acted in November through Resolution 955, it set up a process that the Rwandan government could not accept, forcing Kigali to rely on domestic courts for most trials.

There are a number of reasons that the government of Rwanda could not accept the international Tribunal as the sole mechanism for post-genocide justice.[28] First and foremost, the Tribunal's mandate was only for acts committed during the genocide; all previous planning and conspiratorial activities as well as any actions that "incited" genocide were outside its mandate. Furthermore, the Rwandans objected to a Tribunal with judges that were to be nominated on behalf of countries that had actively supported the previous government and its genocidaires. Resolution 955 was also unacceptable in that it allowed individuals sentenced by the Tribunal to be imprisoned abroad and it ultimately located the Tribunal outside of Rwanda in neighboring Tanzania. From the government of Rwanda's point of view, a Tribunal based in Rwanda broadcast on international news networks was the most promising way to punish violators, engage the international community in the tough work of post-conflict justice, and demonstrate to Rwandan citizenry the political will to bring perpetrators to justice. Moreover, Kigali was also deeply concerned that the UN Security Council set up only a single court of appeals for both the Yugoslav and Rwandan tribunals, and that Resolution 955, unlike Rwandan law, expressly prohibited the death penalty even in the case of the most egregious violators. In the end, many Rwandans identified with the sentiments of Rwanda's UN Ambassador Bakuramutsa, who argued that the Tribunal was a feeble expression of unity with the victims of Rwanda designed to "simply appease the conscience of the international community."[29]

The UN Tribunal will be returned to below. The government of Rwanda decided to press ahead with criminal prosecutions, but had to build a judiciary and related agencies from the ground up, including: importing new lawyers from abroad or training lawyers at university, rebuilding its police, and building prison organizations. And there were numerous juridical questions about the appropriate mechanisms for justice. Olivier Dubois writes, "For instance, how to ensure justice which respects the rights of the individual, with so many suspects, while ruling out an amnesty? What forum to choose for trying such persons: emergency courts, specialized chambers within existing courts, or assize courts? What law to apply so that the specific nature of the crimes committed can be recognized: the direct application of international law, the inclusion of the crime of geno-cide and crimes against humanity in the penal code, or a specific law? How to avoid being accused of violating the principle of non-retro-activity of criminal law?"[30] Rwanda passed a specific law defining the period of genocide and crimes against humanity on August 30, 1996: "The Organization of Prosecutions for Offences constituting the Crime of Genocide or Crimes against Humanity committed since

October 1, 1990 through December 31, 1994" (Organic Law No. 08/96).[31] Four classes of violators were defined:

CATEGORY 1:

a) person whose criminal acts or whose acts of criminal partici-pation place them among the planners, organizers, instigators, supervisors and leaders of the crime of genocide or of a crime against humanity;

b) persons who acted in positions of authority at the national, prefectoral, communal, sector or cell level, or in a political party, [. . .] or fostered such crimes;

c) notorious murderers who by virtue of the zeal or excessive malice with which they committed atrocities, distinguished themselves in their areas of residence or where they passed;

d) persons who committed acts [of] sexual torture;

CATEGORY 2:

persons whose criminal acts or whose acts of criminal partici-pation place them among perpetrators, conspirators of accom-plices of intentional homicide or of serious assault against the person causing death;

CATEGORY 3:

persons whose criminal acts or whose acts of criminal partici-pation make them guilty of other serious assaults against the person;

CATEGORY 4:

persons who committed offences against property.

To give a sense of scale, nearly 2,000 people were indicted under the first category; over time the Rwandan prison system would house close to 120,000 alleged violators and criminals.

What makes the Organic Law unique is that it included an inno-vative mechanism that was intended to induce apologies to victims and confession of crimes, and support speedy justice. This plea-bargaining system exchanged a complete confession—including apology and a listing of accomplices—for major reductions in the sentences. According to one observer, "By encouraging a plea of guilty, the mechanism absolves the court from having to provide evidence against the accused and allows it simply to determine the penalty after verifying the legality and sincerity of the confession . . . [and] sentences are considerably reduced in relation to those that might have been expected under the Penal Code."[32]

The Rwandan justice system faced almost insurmountable hurdles over the course of the next decade, and was helped at many junctures by external actors, including foreign governments and NGOs such as Lawyers Without Borders. In its first year, the system handed down 142 judgments involving the genocide, including sixty-one death penalties and six acquittals. According to Human Rights Watch, this system prosecuted approximately 10,000 individuals over the next ten years—no small accomplishment.[33] However, this system was simply overwhelmed by decade's end, with an estimated 100,000 prisoners in Rwanda's grossly overcrowded prisons and the parallel UN Tribunal process working at an even slower pace.

The Rwandan government found the pursuit of Justice to be just one of its pressing priorities in the aftermath of the genocide: this was a case of nation-building institutions from the ground up. All of the efforts at reconstruction, development, and law enforcement were under the shadow of national security concerns, including the constant threat of renewed violence by exiled interahamwe living just over the border in neighboring Democratic Republic of Congo. So, seven years after the genocide, the government of Rwanda decided to initiate a pilot program of authorizing local gacaca courts ("grass courts") to assist in the unfinished business of national Justice.[34]

In 2004 Kigali began to implement a nation-wide system of local courts under the National Gacaca Courts Service (SNJG).[35] The jurisdiction of gacaca courts did not extend to those crimes being handled by the ICTR and the highest categories of offense under the Organic Law, but this still left tens of thousands of offenders—both in and out of the prisons—to be dealt with under the gacaca system. By 2005 the country boasted 12,000 of these courts, and the system continued to grow over the next several years.[36]

What is a gacaca court? Gacaca refers to a mown lawn where village patriarchs sit to hear disputes and render judgments. The goal of traditional gacaca courts is the realization of a local form of justice that meets the needs of the community, both for Justice and for restored relationships lest a cycle of violence enervate the community. The government, floundering under the number of prisoners and trials awaiting judgment, turned to gacaca as an alternative form of Justice. Under the national program, members of the gacaca courts were elected by their community (thus allowing younger people and women to participate) and were to receive some basic training in Rwanda's criminal justice system. The courts could impose stiff prison sentences, but also had greater latitude in assigning hard labor, community service, and forms of restitution. In practice, lawyers were excluded: the gacaca mechanism was the accused coming forward to admit culpability or claim innocence in the presence of an open assembly of victims and witnesses.

The gacaca system formally closed in June 2010 after trying over 1.5 million cases. It has been the subject of analysis from many quarters, not only for its punishment and restitution components, but also as a method of transitional justice (as described in chapter six) and in terms of national reconciliation. The relative success of the gacaca system will be fully understood only over a period of years, but at present it seems clear that this initiative sustained the larger legal framework, buttressed domestic security and the political order, and reinforced the critical principles of justice and accountability in ways that were pragmatic. At the same time as the efforts of the

Rwandan government to shore up Rwandan security and promote justice, a parallel international court was meeting, and at this writing continues to sit, in chambers in nearby Arusha, Tanzania: the UN-authorized International Criminal Tribunal for Rwanda.

## THE INTERNATIONAL CRIMINAL TRIBUNAL
## FOR RWANDA

On November 8, 1994, the UN Security Council created the International Criminal Tribunal for Rwanda (ICTR) by Resolution 955. At the time, it had only been five months since the end of the genocide that left up to 800,000 Rwandans dead and millions displaced. The situation remained desperate and volatile.[37] In Resolution 955, the Security Council asserted:

> Determining that this situation continues to constitute a threat to international peace and security,
>
> Determined to put an end to such crimes and to take effective measures to bring to justice the persons who are responsible for them,
>
> Convinced that in the particular circumstances of Rwanda, the prosecution of persons responsible for serious violations of international humanitarian law would enable this aim to be achieved and would contribute to the process of national reconciliation and to the restitution and maintenance of peace,
>
> Believing that the establishment of an international tribunal for the prosecution of persons responsible for genocide and the other above-mentioned violations of international humanitarian law will contribute to ensuring that such violations are halted and effectively redressed,
>
> Stressing also the need for international cooperation to strengthen the courts and judicial system of Rwanda, having regard in particular to the necessity for those courts to deal with large numbers of suspects.

The Resolution makes several important arguments about justice, punishment, and reconciliation. The first is that the instability and uncertainty in Rwanda continued, at the writing of the document in late 1994, to be a threat to international peace and security. Indeed, the Security Council had acted under its authority under Section VII of the UN Charter, which states: "The Security Council shall determine the existence of any threat to the peace, breach of the peace, or act of aggression and shall make recommendations, or decide what measures shall be taken in accordance with Articles 41 and 42, to maintain or restore international peace and security."[38]

A critical second point in the Resolution is the determination to, once and for all, "put an end to such crimes and to take effective measures to bring to justice the persons who are responsible for them." The 1994 genocide in Rwanda, tragically, was not an aberration—it was routine, but on a greater scale. Ethnic cleansing was part of life in Rwanda from the overthrow of its last Tutsi king, assumption of Hutu power, and independence from Belgium in 1959–1962 (resulting in at least 150,000 Tutsi refugees and countless dead), through the ethnic-based civil war that culminated in the failed Arusha Accords (1992) and impotent UN mission headed by General Romeo Dallaire. Neighboring Burundi lost 50,000 people to similar violence in 1993; an estimated 3 million died during associated violence in neighboring Democratic Republic of the Congo between 1996 and 2003.

Consequently, the Resolution calls for an end to the cycle of violence and concrete steps to hold individuals accountable for their misdeeds. This is Justice—the idea that individuals are moral agents and thus should be held accountable for their actions. Importantly, the Resolution notes that "the prosecution of persons responsible for serious violations of international humanitarian law" (that is, crimes against humanity) will enable this aim to be achieved—the aim of implementing Justice.

Furthermore, the Security Council asserted that prosecutorial justice "would contribute to the process of national reconciliation and to the restitution and maintenance of peace." How is this the case? As argued in the next chapter, reconciliation is rarely achievable when injustice and insecurity loom. Justice mechanisms, including punishment and restitution, provide a modest satisfaction to the victims by vindicating their rights, by acknowledging evil and criminality, and by punishing wrongdoers. This does not mean that victims' memories of the horror are erased or that lost lives are returned, but it does mean that the new status quo is built on explicit breaks with the old status quo. Hence, in the Rwanda case Justice was a precondition to an ongoing and future environment of peace.

Finally, the Resolution notes the urgent need for international assistance, not only in running an impartial UN-backed tribunal, but in rebuilding the juridical mechanisms of Rwanda itself. Rwanda's courts, prisons, military, and law enforcement agencies were likewise victims of Rwanda's civil war and the genocide, and efforts toward security and justice had regional and international effects. Moreover, as the crimes committed by the Hutu-dominated Habyarimana regime and its interahamwe allies were violations of international humanitarian law, they were literally "crimes against humanity." In other words, by violating the Genocide and Geneva conventions, as well as disrupting the security of the Great Lakes region, the Hutu regime had contravened the ethical mores of international life: it violated its obligations under international law and transgressed the moral fabric not only of Rwandan society but of people everywhere.

As of 2011 it has been over seventeen years since the genocide. What is the record of the ICTR? For many, the Tribunal's exorbitant costs and tiny case load render it farcical. The Tribunal's staff grew at its peak to more than 1,000 people, including judges, historians, prosecutors, defense attorneys, security personnel, researchers, translators, and auxiliaries at a cost in its most recent biennial budget of approximately $125 million per annum. As of this writing it has rendered judgments on forty-four defendants in thirty-five cases from its base in Arusha, Tanzania. There are an additional ten cases with thirty-one defendants in various phases of trial, and ten fugitives remain on the run.[39] According to the ICTR's president, Judge Dennis Byron, the expense is justified: "Equally important, the Tribunal has established a judicially verified factual record of the events in Rwanda that will serve as a background for the remaining trials, a resource for historians, and a major contribution to the process of reconciliation."[40]

So the Court has enforced international law, highlighted gross criminality and wrongdoing, and punished some of the high-level perpetrators. It has heard from witnesses—some of whom were endangered by giving evidence—and established a historical record of events beyond the spin of any single government. Moreover, it has paralleled and thus supported local justice efforts in Rwanda's courts which are supported by tens of millions of dollars invested by the international community. The history and limitations of Rwanda's domestic legal infrastructure and its novel gacaca courts, which have tried over a million cases and were scheduled to terminate in the summer of 2010 (the deadline has been pushed back to December 2011) have been reported on elsewhere.[41] However, what is important is that the ICTR, by taking on senior military and political officials, took some of the pressure off of the local judicial system. Nonetheless, its massive budget and lumbering timeline, particularly when compared with local efforts in Rwanda, seem grotesque. This state of affairs demonstrates the tensions between Order and Justice on the one hand, and some of the conceptual and practical dilemmas of drawn-out, "innocent until proven guilty" judicial processes on the other.

Finally, many feel that the ICTR and its sister tribunal, the International Criminal Tribunal for the Former Yugoslavia (ICTY) reestablished principles of global Justice first articulated, but afterward neglected, at the Nuremberg trials a half-century earlier.

Undoubtedly, these ad hoc tribunals were prototypes for the writers of the Rome Statute in creating the International Criminal Court in 1998. It is thus noteworthy that the ICTR's progeny, the ICC, has before it today four cases—all of which deal with the crimes of individuals in countries near Rwanda: Uganda, the Democratic Republic of the Congo, and Sudan.[42]

### JUSTICE AND RECONCILIATION IN RWANDA

In retrospect, one of the important aspects of post-war Rwanda is that Justice was nested in Order. More specifically, the RPF decisively beat the Hutu-majority army and genocidaires on the battlefield and drove them from the country. The RPF dominated Rwandan political institutions over the next decade, forging and institutionalizing a secure peace on the ground with absolutely no tolerance for destabilizing affronts. In order to keep those enemies, many based in Eastern Congo after 1994, out of Rwandan affairs a series of armed expeditions were mounted to ensure that Rwanda never faced a threat from them again. Moreover, the RPF-dominated government launched numerous initiatives, supported by the international community, to build a robust political, economic, and social order that has made Rwanda the rising power in its neighborhood.

Neither the Rwandan government nor the international community chose the amnesia approach to this conflict. The point to "remembering" was, in part, to reinforce the principles of humanity and morality through the procedures of law and justice. Many of the perpetrators who lived beyond the conflict were punished in some way, whether through local gacaca courts, lengthy prison terms, or more significant penalties such as incarceration for life.

When it comes to the principle of deterrence, it is clear that the powerful security apparatus developed by Paul Kagame and his government is, in part, an instrument of deterrence toward any form of Hutu revanchism. That being said, are the justice mechanisms in Rwanda—either domestic ones or those of the ICTR—deterrents to future ethnic violence? Probably not. It has been documented that some genocidaires, upon leaving Rwanda's prisons, have been undeterred from going home to wipe the slate clean and finish off any last survivors who might testify against them in future, formal court proceedings. Similarly, it is hard to imagine that the ICTR has had any deterrent effect on mass violence perpetrated by state authorities on the African continent. After fifteen years and a tab in the billions of dollars, the fact that only a few dozen high-level perpetrators have been dealt with is a sore spot with many Rwandans and a learning point for authoritarians everywhere that international justice mechanisms are rare, sluggish, procedurally complex, and focused on a narrow set of high-level state representatives.

Did Justice avenge the victims? Did it avenge the suffering of survivors bereft of homes, family members, and their own physical and mental health? Did Justice compensate the survivors in some way? Did Justice pave the way for reconciliation?

Certainly, on the battlefield and in subsequent raids in East Congo, the RPF punished the members of the former Rwandan army and militias responsible for the killing. Through that victory and the imprisonment of thousands of perpetrators and suspects, it took the first steps toward righting past wrongs and punishing those responsible. There have been efforts to provide compensation to the survivors, with the most important being humanitarian and development monies which have come to Rwanda from the international community, in large part due to a sense of collective international guilt that nothing was done to stop the killing in 1994. These funds are weak amends for suffering: they can neither buy off the grief and loss of victims and survivors nor are they a real punishment of the perpetrators—it is not the assets of the thousands of genocidaires that foot the bill.

What about reconciliation? It is entirely possible that many readers are frustrated by this account's choice to exclude the concept of reconciliation—one that is clearly associated with elements of the gacaca process. However, in the uncertain, painful years that followed the 1994 genocide, the deliberate policy of the RPF-dominated government was security and justice. Indeed, for years the official policy of the government was to avoid the very word "reconciliation." The concept was distasteful to a public that had seen a tenth of its population bludgeoned to death by their neighbors with machetes and clubs. As stated in a memo from the UN High Commissioner for Refugees, "The attitude of the government in the years following the genocide was to insist on the need for Justice. The word 'reconciliation' was taboo for those who had survived the genocide, and was never publicly used."[43] It took more than a decade for senior RPF officials to really begin to talk about "reconciliation."

According to Filip Reyntjens and Stef Vandeginste, this sentiment was shared by both local citizens and government officials. The former equated "reconciliation" with "amnesty," and wanted to see justice done. Indeed, the government of national unity's stated objectives were "accountability, justice for victims, and the struggle against impunity."[44] Hence, it was nearly five years before the first steps toward justice-with-reconciliation began, first with an announcement in late 1998 that the government planned to release about 10,000 minor genocide suspects from its overwhelming prison population. With the paroles imminent, victims' groups wanted to ensure that there was some mechanism for accountability, even one rooted in a truth commission if juridical procedures were unavailable. Ultimately, the pilot gacaca program in 2001–2009 was the first step toward a faster-paced, broader process. At the same time, by 1999 it was clear that there was no longer an external threat from Hutus and genocidaires based in Eastern DRC—Rwanda's second intervention in 1998 had demolished any such force. Nor was there a vibrant, destabilizing opposition—the efforts of the former RPF to impose stability were bearing fruit.[45] In short, it took a half-decade following complete battlefield victory and massive efforts at justice—including the incarceration of over 100,000 accused genocidaires—before there was the initial consideration of including reconciliation in the government's programs. And through the entire period of the national gacaca program (2004–2010) and parallel criminal prosecution in Rwandan courts or at the ICTR, all efforts toward Kigali's stated goals of stability, national unity, and justice have expressly avoided any form of political reconciliation with survivors of the former regime or amnesty for the perpetrators. In short, Rwanda, particularly in the first decade of its post-conflict existence, focused on Order and Justice.

## Conclusion

In 2011 Rwanda remains a poor, troubled country but, when contrasted with its neighbors, it is orderly, secure, and has institutions and an economy that are the envy of the region. Following a decisive military victory in 1994, the government invested heavily in basic Order and Justice, intentionally putting off questions of national reconciliation in favor of national unity and security—both principles of Order. In contrast, though action against the government of Saddam Hussein in 1991 and 2003 were putatively designed to bring regional security, the reparations regimes of 1991 and the CPA's "clean sweep" of Iraqi institutions in 2003 contributed to insecurity and disorder. The punishment of Hussein and other senior figures, however, was narrowly targeted, within the rule of law, and justified.

Neither of these is the end of the local story. In 2009, Rwandan president Paul Kagame finally called for something more than national unity: he invited displaced people in neighboring Eastern

Congo—largely Hutus—to return to Rwanda in a spirit of reconciliation. In 2007 Iraq, the military "surge" and "Sunni Awakening," both efforts at finally establishing Order after four years of bloodshed, were supported by highly publicized efforts at reconciliation through the Iraq Interreligious Congress, which included Moqtadr al Sadr and representatives from forty different religious factions, including a representative of Grand Ayatollah Ali Sistani. The public pronouncements by the Congress, summarized in an interreligious document called the Baghdad Accords, buttressed the traditional military and governance efforts toward peace and security. In short, the real-world cases demonstrate that an effective jus post bellum must operationalize a linked, reinforcing regimen of Order and Justice that may be an eventual bridge to Conciliation.

## CHAPTER 5

# Conciliation
## *Coming to Terms with the Past*

From the outset of his presidency, Abraham Lincoln faced the question of how to reunite a fractured nation. The conflict, which unofficially began two months prior to his inauguration with the secession of seven southern states, became a war of attrition lengthier and more appalling than anyone could have imagined. When the South surrendered after four long years, 620,000 troops had been killed and as many as half a million more civilians lay dead.[1]

President Lincoln presided over the war's entire duration. The choices that he and others made ensured that there was no recurrence of warfare, no cycle of violence beyond Appomattox like those witnessed in the Balkans or Africa. Remarkably, some form of reconciliation occurred, setting the U.S. on a path toward prosperity and greatness, despite unresolved issues.

Some of the credit belongs to Lincoln and his associates. Lincoln ever wanted to reconcile the South to the Union; saving the Union was his pole star during the calamitous years of strife. Lincoln directed his battlefield generals at war's end to "let them up easy," to make every possible effort to get the Southern armies to lay down their arms and go home peaceably. He wanted a similar grand reconciliation at the national level, returning some form of Southern representation to the Congress upon oaths of fealty to the government of the U.S.[2]

Perhaps the most dramatic moment of reciprocity to these initiatives was the scene at Appomattox in early April 1865. A series of letters were exchanged between Lieutenant General Ulysses S. Grant, commander of all Union armies in the field, and General Robert E. Lee, commander of the Army of Northern Virginia, on April 7–9, 1865. Grant initiated the dialogue, asking Lee to consider surrender to prevent further bloodshed, "The terms upon which peace can be had are well understood. By the South laying down their arms they will hasten that most desirable event, save thousands of human lives, and hundreds of millions of property not yet destroyed." In a later letter on the same day, Grant spelled out modest terms of surrender, which Lee subsequently agreed to (see box on p. 104).

The encounter at Appomattox culminated in the surrender of Lee's Army of Northern Virginia. Grant avoided brandishing his victory over Lee, and in the days that followed other Southern armies in the field followed Lee's example and surrendered. Jefferson Davis, bereft of all but a small entourage, exhorted the Confederate commanders to take to the hills and instigate a guerrilla war—one that would have taken years, or decades, to eradicate. However, one by one the Southern armies capitulated and Lincoln's plans for national reconciliation seemed to be on track . . . until his death just a week later at the hands of an assassin.

It is beyond the scope of this chapter to identify all the elements of the post-war situation and how affairs proceeded, but were one to fast-forward just a few years one would see how events played out. First and most obvious, national reconciliation proceeded on the basis of a decisive, complete battlefield victory of the North over the South, providing the basis for political order and an imperfect, but stable, security.

Washington provided gradually expanding amnesties in May 1865, December 1868, and again in 1872. A policy of "reconstruction"

April 9, 1865

**General R.E. LEE**

GENERAL: In accordance with the substance of my letter to you of the 8th instant, I propose to receive the surrender of the Army of Northern Virginia on the following terms, to wit: Rolls of all the officers and men to be made in duplicate, one copy to be given to an officer to be designated by me, the other to be retained by such officer or officers as you may designate. The officers to give their individual paroles not to take up arms against the Government of the United States until properly exchanged; and each company or regimental commander sign a like parole for the men of their commands. The arms, artillery, and public property to be parked and stacked, and turned over to the officers appointed by me to receive them. This will not embrace the side-arms of the officers, nor their private horses or baggage. This done, each officer and man will be allowed to return to his home, not to be disturbed by U.S. authority so long as they observe their paroles and the laws in force where they may reside.

**U.S. GRANT,**

Lieutenant-General.

imposed on the South barred Confederate officers and officials from high office and forced a new governing structure on the southern states. There was no systematic punishment or persecution of Confederate loyalists. Jefferson Davis, president of the Confederacy (and a former U.S. senator and secretary of war) was imprisoned at Fort Monroe, Virginia, for two years and released on a $100,000 bond paid by Horace Greeley, Cornelius Vanderbilt, and others. Ultimately

Davis benefited from the narrow amnesty of 1868; all charges were dropped against him in February 1869. Ulysses S. Grant became president a month later, and in 1872 signed a comprehensive general amnesty that removed all remaining restrictions on Confederate soldiers and officials with the exception of a group of the senior-most Confederates. Reconstruction ended in 1876 as a result of political compromise.[3]

President Grant went on to serve a second term. Jefferson Davis headed a life insurance company in Memphis, Tennessee. Robert E. Lee became president of what is today Washington and Lee University in Lexington, Virginia. And although it would be a gross exaggeration to suggest that everyone lived happily ever after, they did live. The men and women of the country followed the example of their leaders, doing the hard labor of beating swords into ploughshares.

How are we to understand this extraordinary set of events that resulted in the peaceful reunification of a country? How can we explain the fact that although most civil wars resume within a few years of a settlement, this one did not? And despite the many unresolved issues of the war, most notably race relations and the future of southern political institutions, not to mention the destruction of the South's economy and the penury of its populace, there was never again to be the real prospect of Confederate revolt. Why not?

Some of the answers to these questions can be found in careful efforts at national reconciliation that Lincoln, his subordinates, and his successors attempted to implement. Military victory, national war-weariness, and the refusal of the defeated to play the part of spoilers all were critical dimensions. Nevertheless, Union policies of amnesty, rebuilding, and political inclusion made some form of Conciliation possible among the fractured citizenry. This chapter explores the idea of Conciliation/Reconciliation at and beyond war's end, including the links between Conciliation and the principles of Justice and Order found in earlier chapters and the critical notions of amnesty, forgiveness, and forgetting. This chapter is not, therefore, an examination about efforts to reconcile domestic politics absent war, such as democratic transitions in South Africa, Eastern Europe, Brazil, Argentina, and Chile in recent years. This chapter is about the conditions under which Conciliation happens between belligerents in intra- and inter-state wars, and the relationship of Conciliation to Order and Justice. Contemporary cases such as East Timor and the Egypto-Israeli peace accords demonstrate that rare cases of Conciliation are the most likely strategies to end wars well.

## The Idea of Conciliation in Post-Conflict

### DEFINING CONCILIATION

The idea of Conciliation, when it comes to post-conflict, is linked to other principles of just war theory. Jus ad bellum—just war's calculus for going to war—begins with legitimate authorities acting with right intent. A true post-conflict political arrangement that includes Conciliation will likewise involve political leaders acting on behalf of a secure post-conflict, in contrast to (as an example) seeking a breather before resuming all-out war. Conciliation also acknowledges the role of Justice: there may be decision-makers who caused the aggression in the first place or violators of the war convention (jus in bello) and these deeds often must be accounted for in some way for Conciliation to be able to take root.

Conciliation is rare. A recent survey of 430 war conflict endings found only a couple of dozen instances of "reconciliation events" at conflict's end. And in many cases, those conciliatory events occurred decades after the war ended, as in the case of German chancellor Willy Brandt's penitential gesture at the Warsaw Ghetto memorial a full quarter-century after the close of World War II.

What is Conciliation? What is its relationship to Order and Justice? Strictly speaking, Conciliation is coming to terms with the past. This "coming to terms" is both resignation and resolution—it is "resigning oneself" to a past that cannot be changed while "resolving oneself" that the past alone need not define the present and the future. In a sense, this is what Jean Bethke Elshtain calls "knowing forgetting": "recollecting the past, but not being so wholly defined by it that one's only option is to be executioner or victim . . . rather than an accountable human agent."[4] She goes on say that "to remember and forget" means "a relinquishment of the full burden of the past in order to envisage an altered horizon of expectation for the future."[5] In the politics of war, this Conciliation entails redefining relationships from belligerency to partnership in a shared future of peace and security.

This latter point is important: in the politics of ending wars well, Conciliation's fundamental purpose is to buttress and expand conditions of collective peace and security. The purpose of Conciliation is not personal absolution, private vengeance, or any form of localized, individual forgiveness—although all such are valuable. Rather, Conciliation is a process of securing the peace, enhancing the Order, and in many cases, allowing some expressions of Justice.

David A. Crocker's model of reconciliation emphasizes the arduous and generally sequential phases of Conciliation. He argues that at the end of civil conflict or political violence, "simple coexistence" may be all that is possible—yet it is far preferable to the resumption of civil war or continued oppression. Crocker is most interested in domestic political transitions, so his second phase is "democratic reciprocity": how relations can thaw gradually when all sides participate in, and accept the outcomes of, democratic processes. These first two steps are primarily mechanisms of basic security and order. Third, in some cases reconciliation can transform society. Crocker writes, "comprehensive reconstruction of social bonds between victims and perpetrators" is necessary [for reconcilia-tion]," perhaps including the findings of truth commissions and post-conflict justice.[6]

Of course, it is not the case that Order, Justice, and Conciliation are completely distinct, non-overlapping categories. Instead, they are overlapping and should be reinforcing. As discussed in chapter seven, the ideas underlying these approaches informed policies in Afghanistan in 2002–2004: to destroy terrorist networks and their supporters, recognize the wider patterns of insecurity (three decades of civil war, independent warlords with their own armies, no centralized authority), address such conditions (such as NATO intervention, Provincial Reconstruction Teams, international devel-opment assistance), and attempt a modest national reconciliation in tandem with security and justice efforts. The national reconciliation effort was characterized by a national *loya jirga* (gathering of representatives of different social and cultural groups) and a major disarmament, demobilization, and reintegration (DDR) campaign wherein tens of thousands of former combatants were honorably discharged—regardless of their previous affiliation—to go home as law-abiding citizens. Hence, the political program of the time was, in a nutshell, to pursue international security and justice by defeating the Taliban–al Qaeda nexus, reframe a secure and more just (such as for women and minorities) political order, and institute a modest national reconciliation that would dismantle armed groups and promote political involvement. In the early years of the conflict (2002–2004), these processes were intended to be mutually reinforcing and overlapping.

Thus, the Order-Justice-Conciliation framework is composed of overlapping principles for post-conflict. Of course, neither in the U.S. Civil War nor in the case of Afghanistan was this model perfected. In the American South, the instigators of war felt little direct punishment after the fact, and some of the gross inequalities of race took another century to resolve, despite the implementation of a real post-conflict order and some minimal national reconciliation. Afghanistan has proven even more tenuous, mainly because it is simply impossible to have a one-sided political order and attendant justice and reconciliation—which is precisely what has occurred. Without a complete battlefield victory, as occurred in the U.S. Civil War and recently in Rwanda and Sri Lanka, there can be no one-sided secure post-conflict: all sides have to be parties to end the war well.

## CONCEPTUAL LIMITS OF CONCILIATION

It is important to understand what Conciliation is not. Conciliation, as a principle within a broad political strategy, is not coterminous with specific tactics of political (re)conciliation such as amnesty or DDR. Conciliation is not necessarily forgiveness, if forgiveness is defined as complete absolution and amnesia—"forgive and forget." And Conciliation, in the context of this book, is not a *pre*-war phenomenon. It could be argued, for instance, that Neville Chamberlain's policy with regard to Hitler and the Czech crisis was "conciliatory." Such strategies, be they appeasement like the Sudeten solution or other mediated political outcomes in the absence of war, are not the type of post-conflict scenarios addressed by this book.

Finally, it is important to distinguish levels of analysis in applying Conciliation, consider the different tactics involved in the field, and bear in mind the important role of time.

First, the term "reconciliation" is often confusing in social contexts because of its many dimensions of meaning. In general usage, reconciliation is defined as restoration of broken relationships. This definition of reconciliation presupposes a prior situation of intimacy between those now in conflict—like a fractured marriage or a schism between father and son. It is easy to speak of restoring relationships, although it is difficult to actually do so in practice, when there are prior positive relations that can serve as the foundation for a renewed partnership.

The same holds true, to a lesser extent, in the growing literature on political reconciliation. Almost the entirety of this literature reports on domestic societies where something is shared. In some cases what is shared among the citizenry is a past history of collective citizenship despite recent conflict along class or ideological lines. Hence, in Latin America, efforts at national reconciliation could point to a national identity rooted in the history of throwing off a colonial yoke and a long-time shared national identity. In other cases of domestic reconciliation, it is shared symbols of citizenship, tradition, and the nation which are appealed to in reconciliation. In the South African case, this was Mandela's cry: "We are all South Africans now!" and it was amplified by appeals to the Christian faith to which most blacks and whites adhered.

However, such shared assets, rooted in a collective past, can be hard to find in cases of long-term civil war (such as Sudan) and may simply not exist in inter-state wars. Thus, for our purposes, the principle of Conciliation is narrowly defined as coming to terms with the past and moving forward toward a shared present and future of security. This distinction, drawn from international relations theory, recognizes the different "levels of analysis" in international affairs: the opportunities and limits of individual human beings versus domestic societies versus nations in anarchic (no central government) in international life.[7] The concept of Conciliation/Reconciliation differs at each level, from the personal forgiveness and restitution possible at the individual level, to domestic political transitions, to the treaties that commonly end inter-state wars.

For the purposes of this book, the focus is on war and its aftermath in the cases of intra- and inter-state war. This considerably narrows the field of cases.

A word about tactics. The objective of ending wars well is an enduring, morally satisfying peace although the reality in most places and times is far more modest. Nonetheless, the post-conflict peace will be more satisfying and likely to continue if Conciliation of some sort is achieved. There are a variety of tactics that have been employed in recent post-conflict scenarios: such tactics should be considered prudentially on a case-by-case basis as to their applicability to a given situation. There is a wide range of such tactics from *amnesty* (pardoning former combatants from all responsibility for their past action), *truth-seeking* (recording past violations as a mechanism to move beyond retributive justice), and *disarmament, demobilization, and reintegration* (honorably discharging ex-combatants and re-identifying them as citizens) to *dissolution* (political settlement dissolving former ties, as in the case of the Czech and Slovak republics) and *alliances* (integrating former adversaries into a new strategic relationship, as with NATO and the Warsaw Pact). None of these is the perfect solution in all cases: thoughtful leaders must consider them depending on context.

Finally, time is a critical issue. Our history books are often misleading: the reader routinely finds in the space of a few pages that two countries, formerly mortal enemies engaged in a gladiatorial contest, are subsequent allies. How can this happen in the space of a chapter? This illustrates what is often missing in analyses of Conciliation: the role of national interests and time. States tend to be concerned first and foremost with their fundamental requirements of security. Hence, as the international environment changes over time, their definition of interests—and therefore their definitions of threat, risk, and enemy—is likely to change as well.

Reformatting of interests occurs over time. It took decades for the relations among Scandinavian countries to move from belligerency to conditions that today are labeled "the Nordic peace."[8] The same is true for the relations between the U.S. and Canada, which were antagonistic through the U.S. Civil War and subsequent "Fenian raids" on Canada by former Union soldiers (of Irish descent) in the late 1860s; indeed, both countries developed war plans for dealing with their neighbor as late as the 1920s despite fighting together in the trenches during World War I. The Franco-German rapprochement of the past half-century is remarkable, but it was occasioned by Germany's complete defeat and unconditional surrender, Allied occupation, and especially fear of the Soviet Union.

In sum, Conciliation is coming to terms with the past to the extent that a changed strategy for the present and future is possible. From Confederates setting down their arms to the birth of NATO and beyond, Conciliation can change the trajectory of a country or region. However, the mechanisms may differ in cases of intra-state conflict in contrast to inter-state war.

## JUST WAR THINKING AND FORGIVENESS

Just war thinking has its historical roots in New Testament Christianity, and forgiveness is certainly a key New Testament theme. Indeed, Jesus—while suffering the agony of torture—forgave his murderers. He likewise forgave his supposed friends who deserted and disavowed him. Following Christ's example of divinely inspired forgiveness, the early church continued to preach a gospel of God's love, Christ's atonement, and forgiveness despite Roman persecution and martyrdom. This example has motivated many to choose pacifism, nonviolence, and religiously informed conflict resolution methods to approach conflict and post-conflict.

However, the instances of forgiveness exercised by Christ and his apostles were not political acts. They were individual decisions to forgive. And such forgiveness, blending human choice with spiritual inspiration, is distinctly different from political acts of apology and reconciliation. It is noteworthy that Jesus taught a great deal about what the kingdom of heaven is like—restored relationships between God and humanity and among humans themselves—but neither he nor his disciples called for a revision of the temporal political status quo. This is an important point: unlike the political forms of reconciliation described in this chapter, Jesus' teaching said nothing about Roman tyranny or overthrowing the political system. In fact, Jesus taught his disciples to pay their taxes and he blessed the faith of a Roman centurion.

The just war tradition takes its cue from Jesus' acceptance of the necessity of public order, and especially from the teachings of the apostle Paul on the need for political order, and how it is a reflection of the divine order and principles of justice. As noted previously, Paul wrote about the obligations of rightful authority in Romans 13: 4–5: "For he [the government official] is the minister of God to thee for good. But if thou do that which is evil, be afraid. For he beareth not the sword in vain: for he is the minister of God, a revenger to execute wrath upon him that doeth evil. Wherefore ye must needs be subject, not only for wrath, but also for conscience sake." In short, the guardians of political order have a moral duty to "bear the sword" in order to punish wrongdoing and defend the good.

There has developed in recent years a great deal of literature on the topic of forgiveness, written from religious and secular perspectives. In the case of the Western religious perspectives, the individual choice of Jesus to forgive is often applied haphazardly not only to individuals, but also to tribes, nations, and governments. However, there is no "turn the other cheek" or "forgive and forget" doctrine of forgiveness in the earliest roots of the just war tradition: it is rooted in a different set of collective norms and obligations. Those obligations, and the hope for a better future, begin with principles found in Romans 13 but also available in a wider body of non-Christian and secular literature from Aristotle to Hobbes to Huntington—that Order and Justice are the first steps toward Conciliation.

Does this mean that there is no place for forgiveness in jus post bellum? No. There are forms of political forgiveness—if one means Conciliation—that can contribute to a thicker, more enduring post-war environment. But such forgiveness is unlikely to follow Christ's example: it will be political, not personal, corporate, not individual, public, not private, and limited, not unconditional or unlimited. In short, a just war approach to ending wars well begins with collective considerations of Order and Justice seeking Conciliation whenever possible; individual forgiveness can buttress the peace but is no substitute for corporate political conciliation.

### CONTRASTING MODES OF CONCILIATION: INTER- VS. INTRA-STATE WAR

In an earlier book, *Just War Thinking*, I discussed the numerous dilemmas associated with "reconciliation" at the end of war. One of the critical issues identified, in theory and in practice, was the difference between intra-state and inter-state wars. The former have a capacity for *re*-conciliation because there are elements of a shared past, however weak, that can be the basis for a shared commitment to future partnership toward peace. In contrast, in international life there may be no "re-," that is, no past sense of shared interests or identity upon which to build a future peace. Hence, in international relations, Conciliation will be based on evolving interests:

> Conciliation is future-focused in that it sees former enemies as partners in a shared future. Sometimes, particularly in intra-state conflict, it is reconciliation—building bridges between parties that have some shared past. In international conflict it is more likely that the goal is Conciliation, the mutual effort of both sides to overcome past hostility and reframe the relationship as one of partnership. If the fundamental goals of just war thinking are to promote international security and to protect human life, then Conciliation does this by

ameliorating the conditions that can lead to new or renewed violence ...

Although I believe that reconciliation based on *caritas* (charity, brotherly regard) is important in individual human relationships and can be called on in intra-state conflicts, it is a tricky notion for international affairs.[9] The international system is based primarily on national interests, and unless interests are engaged, Conciliation is unlikely at war's end. In other words, *among states common interests are the basis for conciliation.* In most conflicts, enemies have a history of tension and competition, and have probably fought openly at numerous times in the past. In this scenario, a change in interests is the usual mechanism for Conciliation to be possible.

Conciliation based on evolving interests is not a new idea. Rousseau and Kant both argued for a perpetual peace based, in part, on sovereigns realizing that war was not in their long-term interest.[10] However, in the real world, such relational changes usually take a long period of time (such as US and Canada) and/or may require a shared threat to provide a context for shared interests (such as Cold War France and Germany).[11]

Were one to do a careful survey of the social science and practitioner literature on reconciliation, one would find the conflation of domestic and international reconciliation. However, a closer look would demonstrate that the vast majority of the literature is not at all about international conflicts, but rather about the end of civil war, or non-war pacted transitions from authoritarianism. Indeed, this latter category—including South Africa's transition from apartheid and the transition from military regimes to democracy in Latin America—makes up the vast bulk of this literature. Furthermore, a single case—the painful and inspiring story of South Africa's transition from apartheid and its Truth and Reconciliation Commission—makes up as much as half of the entire body of literature on political reconciliation over the past 20 years.

What is largely missing, then, are analyses focused specifically on war, and critical examinations of the differences suggested in *Just*

*War Thinking:* distinctions between the mode and mechanisms for Conciliation between civil wars and international conflict. This chapter focuses on Conciliation as a desirable method and end state of jus post bellum. Conciliation actions can lay the groundwork for a satisfying enduring peace. Conciliation in the context of political order itself can be regarded as an end state, as war ending well.

In their recent article, "War and Reconciliation," William J. Long and Peter Brecke provide a useful way to distinguish the different modes of reconciliation in civil conflicts and international wars. Long and Brecke looked at over 400 wars including 109 countries to come up with a data set of post–World War II "reconciliation events." They define a reconciliation event as a formal, public event indicating a desire for improved relations. They found 32 cases of civil conflict or international wars that had some form of reconciliation event, and the authors analyzed whether or not such events decisively contributed to long-term peace and security. What they found was evidence that reconciliation can aid in conclusively ending war, but that the modes and methods of reconciliation in civil conflict were very different from those in inter-state war.

In cases of civil conflict, Long and Brecke identified eleven cases (ten countries) between 1957 and 1993 where a *forgiveness model* of reconciliation helped secure the peace. Their definition of civil conflict is important: "purposive and lethal violence among two or more social groups pursuing political goals . . . with at least one belligerent group organized under the command of authoritative [government] leadership" resulting in "at least 32 people killed within a one-year period."[12] Thus, their cases involve not only traditional civil wars, such as Colombia and Mozambique, but also the violence associated with military regimes in Argentina, Uruguay, and Chile as well as apartheid-era South Africa. Long and Brecke write, "with regards to civil conflicts . . . reconciliation events restore lasting social order when they are part of a forgiveness process characterized by truth telling, redefinition of the identity of the former belligerents, partial justice, and a call for a new relationship. The forgiveness model, however, does not explain why or how international reconciliation events contribute to successful conflict resolution between . . . nations." More specifically, the authors argue that reconciliation events, such as an official apology, speech, visit, handshake, or other action can be a part of a wider process of political forgiveness and social healing for former adversaries.

In civil conflicts, the "reconciliation events" are perhaps better understood as processes over time, usually a mixture of truth-telling (such as a "Never Again" document or public apology) and some form of amnesty. It is noteworthy that Long and Brecke's cases include four failures when reconciliation events did not result in long-term peace (Colombia, North Yemen, and Chad in 1971 and separately in 1993) and only seven successes (Argentina, Uruguay, Chile, El Salvador, Mozambique, South Africa, and Honduras).

Long and Brecke argue that the logic of international wars is quite different. Because the adversaries are not living on top of one another in a shared territory, there are numerous reasons why they "lack the motivations and mechanisms" for the forgiveness model to apply. Hence, reconciliation events are not societal reconciliation, but rather signals of good intentions in a bargaining process, and they usually occur years or even decades after the hot war has ended.[13] More specifically, Long and Brecke's *signaling model* derives from rational choice theory: "costly, novel, voluntary, and irrevocable signals" can result in improved relations, a turning point away from past hostility.

An example of the signaling model is Willy Brandt's *Ostpolitik*, and more specifically the moment when he knelt before the Warsaw Ghetto Uprising monument in Poland. The sight—televised globally—of the West German chancellor kneeling in respect at this place of German atrocity was a powerful demonstration of respect and political contrition. Another example, discussed below, is Anwar

Sadat's speech before the Israeli Knesset calling for a change in relations. In each case, the outreach was innovative and potentially costly—vast swaths of both domestic constituencies were stunned and outraged by these acts. In both cases, the actions were voluntary, not coerced, and they were irrevocable—they could not be taken back or disclaimed. Both resulted in subsequent improvements of relationships and ultimately formal treaties resolving some, though not all, of their conflicts.

Again, it is noteworthy that out of 430 cases of conflict since World War II that Long and Brecke came up with less than three dozen discrete cases of reconciliation. This reinforces the point that just getting to Order is hard; Justice and Conciliation are quite rare. However, Long and Brecke's work also suggests that reconciliation events can contribute to long-term security, particularly at the end of some civil wars. But at least two other points stand out. The first is that it is clear from their cases that the driving feature of post-conflict reconciliation is a shared interest in peace and security. This is true in civil conflicts; when war-weariness combined with changing conditions and international pressure makes national peace under new arrangements desirable for many across sectors of society. It is even truer in international life, when the evidence suggests that changing interests over years or decades in a changing international landscape best help us understand Conciliation efforts. It is to these actual cases we now turn: the cold peace between Israel and Egypt formalized at Camp David (1978–1979) and post-conflict Justice and Reconciliation following East Timor's independence referendum in 1999.

## Conciliation in International Conflict: Egypt and Israel

Today one could hardly say that relations between Israel and its neighbors are pacific. Nonetheless, there has not been an outright war between Tel Aviv and a neighboring government in two decades. Moreover, the largest Arab state—Egypt—has formally been at peace with Israel for thirty years. This is particularly remarkable when one recalls that Egypt and Israel were in a constant state of war for the previous thirty years. What changed? How did this modest Conciliation come about? What can we learn from the Begin-Sadat Conciliation and the resulting Camp David accords that we can apply to other arenas of long-standing international conflict?

In 1948 Egypt, along with Syria, Iraq, and Jordan, attempted to overwhelm the fledgling Jewish state. Israel miraculously survived, and eight years later (1956) invaded the Sinai in tandem with England and France in response to Egypt's nationalization of the Suez Canal. Although this short war, dubbed "the Suez crisis," is generally labeled as a last gasp of European imperialism, for the Egyptians and Israelis it was all-out war, because Egypt's policy upon nationalization of the Suez Canal was to block Israeli access to the Straits of Tiran, and thereby deny Israel's only point of access to the Red Sea. A third war in 1967 pitted Egypt, Syria, and Jordan against Israel. In this case, Israel acted preemptively against military forces massing on its borders, ultimately winning the Golan Heights, the West Bank, the Sinai peninsula, eastern Jerusalem, and the Gaza strip as buffer zones. Its humiliated neighbors attacked again, on the holiest day of the Jewish calendar (Yom Kippur, the Day of Atonement) in October 1973, pushing Israeli forces deep into Israel before the Israeli armed forces once again pushed the invaders outside the country. In each case, Israel saw itself as the victim; its neighbors claimed to be acting on behalf of Arab (and Palestinian) interests.

With this scenario of recurring, violent conflict in mind it is difficult to imagine that six years after the 1973 war Israel and Egypt would sign a comprehensive peace treaty and the leaders of the two states would be awarded the Nobel Prize for Peace. How could such Conciliation occur? What is the nature of this Conciliation? Is this forgiveness, brotherhood, and friendship, or something different? And how has this Conciliation endured?

An important, and often overlooked, part of the context is the way the international environment changed between 1973 and the first steps toward Conciliation in November 1978. Whereas in previous conflicts, the Egyptians had counted on some support from the Soviet Union, by 1977 that support had waned. Indeed, Egyptian president Anwar Sadat feared the Soviets had clandestinely supported mass riots in Cairo in early 1978. He also saw the building of Soviet-funded surveillance systems on Libyan soil as a provocative act—and he acted decisively to destroy them. Following airstrikes on Libyan military installations Sadat flatly stated, "We broke the rule: we attacked a brother Arab country,"[14] but this was due to a changing international environment. And nothing changed more in international relations in 1976 than the transition from the party of Richard Nixon (under Ford's presidency) to that of newly elected U.S. president Jimmy Carter. Carter was the first U.S. president to call for what was understood to be an independent Palestinian state.

In this changed international context, Sadat—the man who in early 1977 said, "As long as there is an Israeli soldier on my land (such as Sinai), I am not ready to contact anyone in Israel at all"[15]—told the Egyptian Parliament on November 9, "There is no time to lose. I am ready to go to the ends of the earth if that will save one of my soldiers, one of my officers, from being scratched. I am ready to go to their house, to the Knesset, to discuss peace with the Israeli leaders."[16]

On November 14 President Sadat confirmed his willingness to sit down with the Israelis in a live television broadcast with CBS's Walter Cronkite. Immediately, the government of Israel provided an official invitation to Sadat, who journeyed to Israel a week later.

For those unfamiliar with this history, one might suspect that Israel was at that time in the hands of dovish politicians. Surprisingly, however, in early 1977 Israel's Labor party lost national elections, ending a quarter century of rule. Menachem Begin's right-wing Likud party took over. Begin and his allies were the last people an observer would have expected to act for peace: Begin led the Irgun during Israel's quest for independence, he had long led a right-wing, minority party in the Knesset, he supported robust Israeli military and settlement policies that grew the 1948 borders to include "Judea and Samaria," including Jerusalem as national capital and annexation of lands taken in the 1967 war. Following the Camp David Accords, it was Begin who authorized the 1982 invasion of Lebanon and the bombing of Iraq's Osirak nuclear facility. Begin was no dove, but he turned out to be a fitting partner for Sadat—himself a former member of the military.

On November 20, 1977, Sadat made a famous speech to the Israeli Knesset calling for peace between the countries.

> How can we achieve a durable peace based on justice? In my opinion, and I declare it to the whole world, from this forum, the answer is neither difficult nor is it impossible despite long years of feuds, blood, faction, strife, hatreds and deep-rooted animosity . . .
>
> You want to live with us, in this part of the world.
>
> In all sincerity I tell you we welcome you among us with full security and safety. This in itself is a tremendous turning point, one of the landmarks of a decisive historical change.
>
> We used to reject you. We had our reasons and our fears, yes.
>
> We refused to meet with you, anywhere, yes. We were together in international conferences and organizations and our representatives did not, and still do not, exchange greetings with you. Yes. This has happened and is still happening . . .
>
> Yet today I tell you, and I declare it to the whole world, that we accept to live with you in permanent peace based on justice. We do not want to encircle you or be encircled ourselves by destructive missiles ready for launching, nor by the shells of grudges and hatreds.
>
> I have announced on more than one occasion that Israel has become a fait accompli, recognized by the world, and that

the two superpowers have undertaken the responsibility for its security and the defense of its existence. As we really and truly seek peace we really and truly welcome you to live among us in peace and security.[17]

Within just a few months, U.S. president Jimmy Carter was leading peace talks at the presidential retreat, Camp David, in the hills of Maryland outside Washington, D.C. What ultimately developed stunned the world: a two-part peace agreement that resulted in a formal peace treaty between Israel and Egypt in 1979. The Camp David Accords were in fact two separate agreements, the first on Israeli-Egyptian relations (such as the Sinai, Red Sea access) and the second on Palestinian issues. As noted above, not only were the treaties signed by Cairo and Tel Aviv, but their significance led to the Nobel Prize for the Camp David leaders.

It is important to note, however, the content of President Sadat's message and what was truly involved at Camp David, as well as what did not occur. In his address to the Knesset, Sadat argued that Israel and its neighbors could "win together" rather than fight mutually destructive, zero-sum wars in the future. Sadat comforted the bereaved and called on citizens to make their voices heard for peace. However, Sadat never gave an inch of ground as to Egypt's prerogatives, nor did he issue any form of apology for Egyptian aggression. In the speech he asserted that in order to "end the state of belligerency in the region," Israel must return the lands seized in the 1967 war. In other words, despite the attack on Israel in 1967 and in 1973, Egypt, Jordan, and Syria did not see their losses as Israel's legitimate spoils of war—but rather a form of unjust occupation mirroring Israel's treatment of the Palestinian population. Sadat referred to the "unfortunate" series of conflicts beginning in 1948, but he conceded no Egyptian responsibility for any of them. The speech was stern yet visionary stuff about the present and the future, but it could not in the least be misconstrued as an apology for past violence or a request for forgiveness.

The result, as well known, was the Camp David Accords and subsequent treaties. Both sides chose to end the "state of war" that had formally existed since 1948. Israel gained what it had long sought—official recognition by the most powerful state in the Arab world. Israel also received public assurances that the Straits of Tiran and other nearby waterways would be completely open to international commerce, and of course, Israel could expect that its "good behavior" would continue to be rewarded tangibly by Washington. Egypt also won: after losing the Soviets as a patron it gained the U.S., a financial arrangement that continues to this day. Egypt, unlike its neighbors, saw its lands restored. And Egypt catapulted to a new prominence in international affairs at the same time that Afghanistan, Iran, Saudi Arabia, and other countries in the region were facing unprecedented challenges.

Long and Brecke call Sadat's speech a "reconciliation event," which they define as "costly, novel, voluntary, and irrevocable signals" for peace. Sadat's declaration that he would go to Israel, stated not only before Egypt's parliament but also on international television with Walter Cronkite, was voluntary (it surprised even his wife), innovative, and potentially costly—none of his advisers wanted him to go to Israel. The content of his speech was likewise novel and potentially costly—his rivals at home derided the speech as weak and cowardly. The argument for peace was irrevocable; he could not disclaim it. And who would have imagined that Menachem Begin, the lion of Israel's political right since before independence, would "open" Egypt? Begin's political hand was even weaker than Sadat's, for he led a government coalition supported by ultra-nationalist and Orthodox parties that had only been in power for months when Sadat first issued his appeal. Begin too was willing to act courageously, and in terms of Israel's interests as he understood them, in a manner that was similarly novel, voluntary, potentially costly, and irrevocable.

Was this reconciliation? No. This was not the resumption and healing of a broken relationship. However, it was Conciliation—coming to terms with the past and working together toward a changed future. The state of Conciliation between Israel and Egypt has never been warm and congenial, but it has endured a cold peace without a resumption of war for over three decades.

## Justice and Reconciliation in Intra-State Conflict: East Timor

### UN INTERVENTION IN EAST TIMOR (1999)

The Portuguese empire disintegrated in 1974–1975 following a Socialist coup in Lisbon. Whereas most of its possessions in Africa and Asia gained independence (Angola, Mozambique, Cape Verde, Sao Tome, and Principe), the diminutive colony of East Timor was annexed by neighboring Indonesia. East Timor suffered and suffered under conditions of brutality for a quarter-century until a UN-sponsored referendum in 1999.[18] That referendum ultimately led to nominal independence under a UN Transitional Administration for East Timor (UNTAET) until full sovereignty as Timor-Leste in 2002.[19]

The year of the referendum, 1999, was violent and chaotic. Jakarta supported a policy of intimidation, but 80 percent of the local populace nonetheless voted for independence. The violence perpetrated by the Indonesian military, police, and especially local armed militias resulted in the deaths of over a thousand people, the destruction of private and public property, and the displacement of hundreds of thousands of people.[20] Sexual violence, arson, and torture were commonplace.[21]

The East Timor case is illustrative of the fundamental approach this book takes to ending wars well. The processes were rooted first and foremost in a strategy for imposing and securing Order in East Timor. The Australia-led Intervention Force for East Timor

(INTERFET) muscularly entered a chaotic environment. It has become a model for subsequent interventions because, unlike most of its UN-sponsored predecessors, the blue helmets had a robust mandate to impose security—and used it. The rules of engagement allowed for greater use of force, curfews, forced disarmament, and other measures that put to shame the toothless measures employed by UN peacekeepers at Srebrenica and Kigali. And the bulk of military forces were first-rate, modern combat troops from Australia supported by Thais, South Koreans, and others—not barefoot privates from poor countries.

James Cotton writes, "INTERFET's relative success can be attributed to the rapid insertion of overwhelming force in a context where the political ground had been very carefully prepared."[22] That political ground refers to work at the UN and in national capitals—especially Canberra—on the legal basis for and boundaries on the intervention. Moreover, that attention to detail resulted in an occupation authority, the UN Transitional Authority for East Timor, which was set up to guide the country to full sovereignty in 2002.[23]

What makes the East Timor case unique is that the intervention did not end with stopping the killing. As in Kosovo there was some political will in the region to fund and develop the reestablishment of government structures and basic services. What makes East Timor unique, however, are the overlapping yet distinct strands of Justice and Conciliation activities in civil society and government.

## GRASSROOTS JUSTICE AND RECONCILIATION (2000–)

Dionisio Babo-Soares, a local government official and scholar in East Timor, has documented the cultural mechanisms for reconciliation which began to act in 2000. The date is important because the violence occurred with the September 1999 referendum; the official

UN-authorized truth and reconciliation commission was not authorized until two years later. In the meantime, however, local processes were already under way which laid the groundwork for reconciliation.

Babo-Soares writes that *nahe biti* ("rolling out the mat") is a Timorese process of reconciliation with "a stable social order in the community as its ultimate goal."[24] He describes the custom of consensus and reconciliation thus: "The process emphasizes a number of aspects . . . willingness to come together, to accept culpability, to reach consensus with one's adversaries, and agree to disagree in order to maintain the social order."[25] This grassroots reconciliation was a critical first step to social stability and reconciliation. The process became increasingly institutionalized in local panels hearing individual acceptance of culpability, judgments of community service, and ultimately acceptance back into the community.

The situation in late 1999 was dire: tens of thousands of East Timorese had neighbors and relatives who had fled across the border to West Timor and were living uncertainly in refugee camps. Thousands of those who had fled East Timor were implicated in wrongdoing in the home communities and feared reprisal, however; the situation of mass displacement and fear of retribution made the long-term situation untenable. What ended up occurring were dozens, and later hundreds, of efforts at reconciliation by families and community leaders to resolve the situation. This began through cautious communication between families on both sides of the border, a series of meetings resulting in formal arrangements for return of those individuals who had left, and generally a ceremonial welcoming back that includes a public confession of guilt. In some instances a UNTAET representative was present. A panel of citizens and local officials heard the admissions and assigned some form of restitution or community service for low-level violations; of course, graver crimes were handed over to government authorities.

Observers of this process indicate that it predated the implementation of the formal UN-supported truth and reconciliation process by over a year and a half, thus establishing a two-track justice and reconciliation model that continued to evolve in East Timor. Most importantly, local traditions of reconciliation rooted in concern for social order, accountability, and peace were implemented and were critical to the success of future formal legal mechanisms in supporting security and justice across the country.

### FORMAL JUSTICE AND RECONCILIATION (2002–2005)

In July 2001, UNTAET established the Commission for Reception, Truth, and Reconciliation in East Timor, one of two parallel instruments for dealing with post-conflict justice and reconciliation. Additionally, UNTAET established East Timor's judicial and legal systems, including four district courts and an appellate court. To complement these courts, UNTAET created a Serious Crimes Investigation Unit (SCIU) and two Special Panels as part of the Dili District Court to deal specifically with crimes during the referendum (January 1–October 25, 1999).[26]

The East Timor situation was unique in its parallel systems for truth and reconciliation on the one hand, and serious crimes on the other. The SCIU and the Special Panels were a juridical model for dealing with "international crimes" including war crimes, torture, crimes against humanity, and genocide as well as murder and sexual offenses. Much of the language setting up the panels (UNTAET Regulation 2000/15) and defining its universal jurisdiction over "international crimes" was taken directly from that of the Rome Statute creating the International Criminal Court. The criminal panels also had local jurisdiction for murder and sexual offenses as defined in the Indonesian Criminal Code and were made up of two international judges and one judge from East Timor.

The Special Panels began their work in January 2001 and within the space of two years issued forty-five indictments covering 140 individuals. Thirty-one people were tried and convicted, with sentences of up to thirty-three years in prison.[27] Nevertheless, the panels have been criticized because of their impotence to reach across the border to arraign members of the Indonesian military and government responsible for many of the atrocities. The Indonesian government, in response to international pressure, set up its own Ad Hoc Human Rights Court on East Timor, which convicted two East Timorese of crimes during the referendum and acquitted nine Indonesian police and military officers. Little additional justice is expected of the Indonesian court.

The Special Panels were a juridical instrument for dealing with the worst crimes in an overwhelming situation: a place where over 1,000 people were killed and as much as half the population (out of a population of about one million) fled their homes. It is an understatement to aver that the post-conflict challenges were great—not simply the prosecution of gross offenders, but also the reestablishment of law and order, provision of basic services, the reintegration of refugees (including many perpetrators), and rebuilding of the economy. Despite all this, the Special Panels did make an effort at justice.

In addition to legal and criminal proceedings, UNTAET established a Commission for Reception, Truth and Reconciliation (CRTR) on July 13, 2001, which ran from 2002 to 2005. Due to the ubiquitous nature of the 1999 violence and the fact that thousands were still in refugee camps, the Commission was given a broad mandate to do two things: establish and document the truth about what happened during the violence, and facilitate acceptance and reintegration. The latter was particularly important because it was estimated that 1–4 percent of the population perpetrated politically inspired offenses such as looting, arson, and destruction. It was believed that not dealing in a formal setting with these individuals would destabilize the fragile situation as refugees returned, but the conviction remained that some form of Justice must bulwark any type of Reconciliation: blanket amnesty and/or amnesia was not acceptable.

The Commission was made up of approximately thirty individuals, including a half-dozen national commissioners and two dozen regional commissioners selected by UNTAET representatives and leaders of various political parties, NGOs, and other groups. CRTR ran hearings to document the experience of victims and had the power to subpoena individuals and to request search warrants from the District Court in Dili. CRTR's purpose was not only to document what had happened but also to make recommendations toward preventing similar human rights violations in the future. CRTR also recommended that gross violations be handed over to the justice mechanisms of the Serious Crimes Investigations Unit and the Special Panels.[28]

The Commission's objective was limited amnesty, reconciliation, and reintegration. Victims provided evidence against perpetrators, and those who had committed crimes had to not only take public responsibility for their violations before the Commission, but also accept a judgment of community service to be completed in their home area via the indigenous processes described earlier. Accepting this mechanism allowed the perpetrator to return home.

In an insightful analysis of CRTR's mission, one scholar argues that the truth commission model is particularly useful in East Timor for a variety of reasons.[29] First, it has an investigative mission that can paint a broader, societal portrait of the conditions that caused the conflict rather than simply focusing on individuals. Second, a truth commission can bring to light those issues and individuals who may not be dealt with in traditional national and international courts—such as Indonesian military officers and government elites. Third, unlike in many criminal trials, victims are the focus: they can be heard and their experiences documented, providing an opportunity for their healing. Finally, in the case of CRTR, this is a "justice-supporting" mechanism designed to reintegrate former combatants and perpetrators into society by formally acknowledging the crime, naming the perpetrators, and forcing them to provide restitution through community service. Although such falls short of more comprehensive justice mechanisms like criminal courts, nonetheless it does provide a process for taking violations seriously while providing for reintegration and reconciliation.

In conclusion, the links between Order, Justice, and Reconciliation are clear in the East Timor case. Order was established and rapid efforts were made to begin processes of Justice. The processes of Justice and Reconciliation were carefully crafted to be mutually reinforcing. Finally, any debates about "top-down" versus "grass-roots" or "international" versus "local" approaches to Justice and Reconciliation are short-sighted: in East Timor all of these approaches were utilized synergistically. East Timor was a particularly volatile place because not everyone supported independence, and thus initiatives along multiple vectors were necessary to promote Justice and Reconciliation.

Finally, the East Timor case should remind us of the many natural limits of even the best of intentions and efforts. East Timor struggled with stability throughout the past decade, formally inviting another intervention by Australia in 2006. It is a tiny, poor quasi-state with a population about the size of Detroit or Birmingham (U.K.)—half the population of the other 1999 intervention "state," Kosovo. It is hard to imagine that East Timor will achieve, in our lifetimes, the capacity or resources to be more than basically self-sufficient, but if it does so it will be in large part due to the establishment of Order and mutually sustaining efforts at modest Justice and sincere Conciliation.

# Conclusion

Just war thinking begins with concerns about how warfare does violence not only to human life, but to human communities. Hence, it calls for restraint, investigates motives and justifications, and seeks wars' endings that establish an enduring peace. The cases of East Timor and Egypto-Israeli peace demonstrate the linkages between the three cardinal principles of this book and how they overlap and reinforce one another. Violence in East Timor resulted in an Australia-led intervention under UN auspices followed by multiple tracks of Justice and Reconciliation at the local and national level. Egypt and Israel determined it was in their interest to end three decades of war following President Anwar Sadat's surprise offer to go to Israel to pursue peace. This olive branch resulted in a new regional Order and a minimal political Conciliation, without Justice or forgiveness, which has nonetheless kept a cold peace for thirty years.

To this point of the book, considerations of Justice and Conciliation have reminded the world that outside the just war tradition there exist other fields and sub-disciplines interested in post-conflict. Many of them have formally emerged over the past two decades. What, then, is the relationship between these new fields and just war? What does just war thinking have to say about transitional justice, human rights law, and conflict resolution? Are these fields, in philosophy or practice, simply the real-world expressions of jus post bellum? Are they something more beyond the tradition? Or, perhaps, are their presuppositions in conflict with just war thinking at war's end? The next chapter examines the connections and contradictions between the jus post bellum model of this and these other fields.

## CHAPTER 6

# Connections and Contradictions
## *Just War Thinking vs. Other Post-Conflict Approaches*

Just war thinking is moral decision-making by political and military actors when deciding how and when to employ military force. The tradition is open to debate and reflection by citizens, scholars, and religious authorities, but its goal is not endless academic disputation—the goal is to allow for informed, moral policy at all stages of conflict. This is not to discount the voice of reflection—just war thinking can be particularly helpful in retrospective consideration of moral issues in past conflicts to inform policy. This book, however, extends just war thinking, from its usual realm of ad bellum and in bello, to analyses of late- and post-conflict issues for the same purpose.

This chapter is about connections, and contradictions, between the just war tradition and other fields. As argued throughout this book, a just war approach to ending wars well must cohere to the just war tradition. Jus post bellum is not simply an amalgam of post-conflict tactics, nor should it be an omnibus package into which we throw all forms of post-conflict activity. Instead, a just war approach to late- and post-conflict focuses on values explicit in the tradition, such as order, restraint, moral agency, and justice. In short, this chapter explores the linkages and limits of just post-war thinking and other fields while avoiding conceptual overstretching.[1]

This idea that there are conflicts between post-war justice and other values is not new. For example, there exists a small, complementary literature that analyzes contradictions between post-war justice and the implementation of liberal democracy. This debate arose from failures in the orthodox post-conflict model of the past generation: imposition of Western-style liberal democracy with funding support for political parties, independent media, and elections regardless of the security conditions on the ground. Martha Minow distinguishes some of these tensions, such as between due process (innocent until *proven* guilty)—even for genocidaires—and swift justice which is in tune with popular opinion.[2] Similarly, Pauline H. Baker pondered whether we can "reconcile the two imperatives of peace: conflict resolution on the one hand, and democracy and human rights on the other . . . Should peace be sought at any price to end the bloodshed, even if power-sharing arrangements fail to uphold basic human rights and democratic principles?" Roland Paris criticizes the "Wilsonian approach to peacebuilding," meaning extensive political liberalization as one of the first activities of post-conflict. Contrary to much of the received wisdom at the UN, Paris (echoing Huntington in chapter three) argues that liberalization (competitive elections, free market economy, among other things) without strong institutions will impede the consolidation of peace. Likewise, Timothy Sisk asserts that "the international community's efforts to promote peace through democracy in traumatized societies have been fraught with peril." He goes on to elucidate how power-sharing arrangements can be inherently destabilizing to new governments, and suggests alternative forms of democratic institutions that can buttress order and, in some cases, promote justice.[3]

The point of this reference to the democracy vs. justice and order literature is not to engage it in depth, but rather that it is suggestive of a series of other connections and contradictions, specifically between the just war tradition and fields related to conflict and post-conflict (such as conflict resolution studies, transitional justice, international law and organizations, humanitarianism, and human rights law). Many of these overlaps and disjunctures have not been fully explored, and, at times, the term "jus post bellum" is thrown into the introductory paragraph of a discourse on one of these fields with no other substantive reference to or foundation in the just war tradition.

This chapter disentangles and analyzes this intellectual milieu. Rather than lumping all of these important fields into a just war approach to post-conflict, this chapter compares the presuppositions and value commitments of each field, distinguishing what is shared with the just war tradition and what is not. The discussion is designed to poke and provoke, forcing us to understand critical differences of approach, philosophical orientation, and practice. Its goal is ultimately to promote the next generation of scholarship and practice on points of contact and departure between jus post bellum and other fields, with the ultimate objective of ending wars well.

## Conflict Resolution

The field of conflict resolution (CR) has grown over the past twenty years to include academic journals, conferences, and Master's degree and certificate programs at major universities. The objective of CR is to resolve conflict in a way that is mutually beneficial for all participants. CR techniques such as mediation and arbitration are applied in a variety of settings, from divorce proceedings to corporate mergers to major conflagrations.

CR's approach is relational—it presupposes that conflict can be resolved through the building of, or healing of, relationships. CR calls upon participants to take responsibility for their own contributions to conflict ("confess one's sins") and put themselves into the "shoes" of their enemy. These elements of humanization and humility, it is argued, are the building blocks for reframing the conflict scenario from zero-sum to mutual gain. Indeed, CR practitioners often advocate an expanded notion of peace—the so-called positive peace—that goes beyond basic state security at war's end, in pursuit of social justice, economic and political redistribution, and significant social change. In the case of war, John Paul Lederach argues that CR practitioners must engage all stakeholders: local citizens, mid-range leaders (such as religious leaders), and national leaders to rebuild relationships. "The efforts to work with counterparts, enemies, across the lines of division" is key, a process Lederach calls "horizontal capacity" to improve relationships. Lederach has recently observed that although building horizontal capacity is difficult, it is even more difficult (and desirable) to build "responsive and coordinated relationships up and down the levels of leadership" (such as grassroots through national leaders) to create an interdependent set of relationships for peace.[4]

Is conflict resolution *jus post bellum*? No, the two are far from synonymous. In fact, there are some important distinctions to be made between them. However, there are insights from CR that are useful tactics when trying to end wars well. Although CR purports to work at the state and inter-state level, the majority of CR practice occurs at the local level. In part this stems from an assumption that grassroots change is likely to shift culture and political structure over time. Such efforts to build local understanding and rapprochement can be valuable, although there is little systematic evidence of the proven utility of CR-related activities in constructing an enduring peace in war-ravaged societies. In part, this may be due to the conceptually confusing array of CR tactics found in the literature and in the promotional materials of CR NGOs, from high-level negotiations to local activities such as volleyball, choirs, puppetry, youth centers, dance teams, and the like. In practice, many CR activities tend to be small, local, and informal and not necessarily reflective of the larger power realities of major conflict. CR advocates may retort that engaging youth via conflict resolution methodologies can change the future, but the social science literature suggests that those youth—when attaining high office as adults—usually act on behalf of the interests of the institutions and constituencies that they represent. In other words, where one sits (community center vs. presidential palace) often dictates one's approach to conflict.

In addition to neglecting structural power realities, which the just war tradition recognizes, CR engagement tends to take a stance of neutrality. To be fair, this is an emerging debate among CR practitioners about whether to consistently define themselves as neutral third-party arbiters whose role is to facilitate relationship building, consensus, and healing. Mediation can be valuable in inter-state wars, such as the diplomacy that earned President Theodore Roosevelt a Nobel Prize in 1905. Roosevelt eschewed traditional diplomacy by directly engaging the Russians and Japanese in talks, without an armistice in hand and to the consternation of diplomats and military officers, to mediate an end to the conflict. In this case, third-party mediation allowed war-weary belligerents (particularly the Russians, who faced civil unrest at home) a chance for peace. However, such mediation—when not backed by security guarantees in insecure environments—seems prone to failure, particularly in the case of civil wars. As Barbara F. Walter has demonstrated, intra-state wars often recur because neither party can completely trust the other side to meet its security commitments. Walter argues that only a robust third-party security guarantor (such as armed peacekeepers) can satisfy this requirement; such is not a role that CR practitioners usually play.[5]

The identification of third-party neutrality is quite different from the approach of just war thinking, with its focus on moral agency and justice. True, many advocates of CR as "peacebuilding" assert the theoretical importance of justice.[6] However, in practice CR usually directs its attention to reconciliation without justice, and may in fact be opposed to justice in some situations. This situation occurs when it is deemed that efforts at justice are expected to inflame further controversy, and therefore not consonant with a spirit of reconciliation. Privileging reconciliation and harmonious relationships contrasts with chapter four's argument that justice mechanisms should not disrupt political order; however, in both CR and just war thinking the resultant policy may be the same—limits on punitive justice.

In short, CR typically tends to focus on building relationships at the local level, generally through neutral intervention by friendly third parties, in pursuit of resolving conflict in the interest of peace. In practice, many of the tools of CR may be useful in pursuing jus post bellum in a specific context, but they are tactics which are part of a larger arsenal of approaches for establishing durable security. Furthermore, the reality is that CR approaches have a weak track record in bringing dictators to the table, stopping civil war, or building regional security in insecure contexts. This is largely due to the narrow, local focus of most CR efforts and the lack of resources inherent in CR to overcome security dilemmas. This is especially true if an empathetic approach to CR begins with not only self-assessment but self-denunciation ("I am guilty of . . . we are guilty of . . .). This is simply a non-starter for most political leaders as well as the constituencies that they represent—particularly if they have a long history of historic grievance. Furthermore, CR has little to say about prosecuting violations of the war convention (jus in bello) in the aftermath of war.

To this point, I have been somewhat critical of CR because the evidence is thin that these approaches have made a difference in ending wars well. The work of CR practitioners often takes place in the most violent of places like Kashmir, Bosnia, and Colombia, but it is unclear that there is a repository of national and regional examples of success at ending wars well. Nonetheless, one well-documented case is that of Mozambique, where religious peacemakers brokered the end to the country's long-standing civil war. In the Mozambique case, Cold War polarity, remnants of colonial antagonisms, and interlocking social, economic, and ethnic differences exacerbated conflict between the leftist FRELIMO government and the RENAMO insurgency. Beginning in the early 1980s the bishop of Beira and the Catholic lay organization Community Sant'Egidio discreetly developed relationships with both sides. Sant'Egidio built trust over the next decade through goodwill gifts of desperately needed humanitarian supplies and private consultations with the government and rebel forces. It took years before the first, unofficial meetings between the belligerents, and the better part of a decade before other governments (including Italy and the U.S.) were included in peace talks. Ultimately, this Christian organization led the way, through dialogue, prayer, relationship-building, and mediation, to formal peace accords that ended Mozambique's civil war in 1992.[7]

The Mozambique case is sui generis: it reminds us of the potential of conflict resolution in warfare, but it is an isolated case, from which it is difficult to extrapolate. In short, CR is simply not jus post bellum, although its tactics may be useful in some specific cases. However, another field—transitional justice—does share some priorities with the just war tradition, particularly the pursuit of justice for human rights violations.

## Transitional Justice

Transitional Justice (TJ) refers to a variety of approaches recognizing victims of human rights violations and promoting justice in the aftermath of political transition. These approaches, rooted partly in human rights advocacy, include activities such as truth commissions, criminal prosecutions, reparations, and amnesty. The moniker "transitional justice" provides insight into the roots and presuppositions of the field, the lived experiences of regime change from authoritarian rule, particularly in South American and Central European societies, during the 1980s and 1990s. The concept of *transition* from authoritarianism to democracy comes from the political science literature. The intellectual context is important for this discussion because most cases of TJ are in situations where national governments were primarily responsible for human rights violations at home, in contrast to grievances perpetrated by external aggressors or sub-state actors. In other words, TJ usually focuses on indigenous regime transition, not on the aftermath of inter-state war.

During the "third wave of democratization" of the 1980s and 1990s many of the transitions were "pacted," meaning that compromises were made between the old guard (who still retained most of the coercive tools of the state) and popular, though weak, forces for change.[8] Such compromises made peaceful political transition possible where it had seemed impossible, although this was often dependent upon some type of amnesty to former agents of the state. Perhaps the most famous case is that of Chile, which provided a blanket amnesty to the regime of General Augusto Pinochet, stacked the judiciary and Senate with his supporters, and provided Pinochet himself with immunity from prosecution for life. The fundamental issue for many justice advocates in cases like Chile, post-apartheid South Africa, or post-Communist Romania is a deep skepticism that democracy can truly be consolidated if festering justice issues are left unresolved.[9]

Transitional justice activities are most often employed not after traditional inter-state war, but in the aftermath of dictatorship or authoritarian government. The focus is not on whether or not the previous regime was representative but on whether systematic violations of human rights occurred. One type of TJ approach is formal criminal prosecution of gross human rights violators. The perpetrators may be low-level, hands-on agents of the state (such as prison guards, rank-and-file military) or the senior leaders responsible for creating the policy which led to the violations. Criminal prosecution is generally under the jurisdiction of national law (such as rape, murder), but may also include violations of international law as well (such as the Geneva or Torture Conventions or Rome Statute). Traditionally, trials have taken place within the country, but, increasingly, there is considerable external assistance available as well, such as foreign government or NGO expertise. For example, as discussed earlier, Rwanda has employed traditional gacaca courts at the local level as well as more traditional national juridical prosecutions in conjunction with a UN Criminal Tribunal which has prosecuted dozens of elite defendants for war crimes in nearby Tanzania. Another example is the Special Court for Sierra Leone, which was set up jointly by the UN and the government of Sierra Leone. The Special Court indicted former Sierra Leonean warlords and government ministers as well as pursuing a judgment against former Liberian president Charles Taylor in a trial at The Hague.

Related to seeking punishment of perpetrators are efforts to recompense victims and their families. The objective is to provide financial restitution for the egregious losses suffered by the family. In most cases, the grievances are so significant that financial remittances can never restore or replace what was lost, although money may provide needed support to a pensioner, a widow, or children. Furthermore, in the context of a national apology, reparations may do some good in vindicating those who have been harmed and are grieving: the symbolic value of the state accepting responsibility for past policies can be an important step forward.

Of course, a poor country, wracked by war, unstable in its political transition and identity, and characterized by weak institutions with little legitimacy, will likely find it difficult to prosecute the outgoing regime or find the capital to provide financial benefits to victims. Hence, TJ has increasingly employed "truth-seeking" mechanisms through "truth commissions" as a form of restitution. The fundamental goal of such initiatives, like South Africa's Truth and Reconciliation Commission, is to publicly document the tragic experiences of citizens. Public testimony of human rights abuses will not alter the past, but it may relieve the hearts of some victims and their families who want to be heard and their loss acknowledged. Furthermore, truth commissions usually publish a documented/ historical narrative of what occurred in order to counter alternative, sterilized historicism about previous "golden eras." In some cases, truth-seeking exposes the external world to the true nature and extent of crimes committed, and truth commissions can elaborate recommendations for reformed institutions and practices in the future (though these are often ignored by governments). Often truth-seeking and truth-recording result in publicly accessible reports as well as public monuments or memorials to commemorate a "Never Again!" message to future generations.[10]

Transitional justice advocates argue that their efforts are designed to break cycles of violence in order to create long-term peace and security. Hence, this collection of activities such as truth-seeking, judicial proceedings, and reparations are often balanced with some form of amnesty. On the one hand, amnesty declarations or platforms of political forgiveness are pragmatic—they can make a pact with the outgoing regime possible. But, with the longer view in mind, TJ suggests that the only way to have long-term stability is through some form of reconciliation. That effort may be very modest, such as deliberate outreach to keep potential spoilers on the path to peace (as with Inkatha in South Africa and senior military leaders in Argentina), or in other cases it may include more deliberate activities to reintegrate former fighters or elements of the regime back into the wider society.

Finally, TJ advocates are increasingly involving themselves in security sector reform (SSR) activities designed to reform, or better transform, the security apparatus of the state. Such programming includes training on universal human rights standards, domestic and international law, and best practices in law enforcement. Reform and professionalization of police, the courts, and the military are critical elements of changing the political structures within a country.

TJ is clearly not jus post bellum, although many of its tactics are likely to be useful in post-conflict. TJ is deeply rooted in evolving domestic politics, whereas jus post bellum is entirely focused on war and peace. When it comes to law, TJ is primarily concerned with human rights under domestic and international law, whereas the just war tradition specifically attends to the laws of armed conflict.

TJ is a product of applied democratic theory, and its proponents tend to favor a single regime type—democracy. Jus post bellum is not democracy-exclusive. The just war tradition is about war in all its varieties; TJ is rarely about bona fide war, instead focusing on domestic political transitions from authoritarian government. In fact, just war thinking is agnostic about regime type, instead focusing on the moral decisions of government leaders—whether democratic or not. An authoritarian regime might fight for a just cause using restraint and appropriate tactics just as a democracy may choose an unjust cause or employ battlefield violence in a way that violates the war convention.

TJ is rooted in human rights principles and domestic laws and therefore is generally about law enforcement, though often in a national and aspirational sense, such as holding ex-tyrants accountable for breaking their own laws. In contrast, jus post bellum is about war itself, usually inter-state war. All of this is not to say that jus post bellum cannot benefit from TJ—it can—but one should be cautious in its application. Too often the simplistic policy recommendation for post-conflict societies is to authorize a Truth and Reconciliation Commission based on the South African model because that is the famous exemplar of success, despite the fact that South Africa did not have an all-out civil war. Indeed, neither did Brazil, Argentina, Chile, or most of the European countries that employed TJ techniques.

So, in the case of intra- or inter-state war, what is the connection between TJ and just war thinking? First, both are rooted in a deep appreciation for the rule of law and both value the mechanisms of justice. These activities, such as criminal prosecutions and reparations, can be useful in the phases of jus post bellum described in this book. Second, especially in cases of armed humanitarian intervention (such as East Timor, Kosovo) which installs a modest peace, separates belligerents, or affirms/asserts a new border, truth-seeking can bring some local relief to citizens when real justice against a neighboring country is unlikely to be achieved. As discussed in the previous chapter, an example where TJ seems to have made a difference on the ground is in East Timor. East Timor was oppressed by Indonesia for a quarter-century and was subsequently decimated following a vote for independence in the referendum of 1999. The UN Transitional Authority for East Timor (UNTAET) and successor government of East Timor employed justice and reconciliation mechanisms, informed by TJ theory, to distinguish between gross violations (such as murder) and minor offenses, ultimately establishing two distinct judicial systems to process different levels of cases. Minor offenses were often "forgiven" upon a declaration of guilt and community service, with the intent of buttressing the peace through truth-seeking, justice, and reconciliation mechanisms. Major offenses followed a different juridical procedure. These activities, in tandem with efforts to found an enduring and safe political order, are jus post bellum in practice.

## Human Rights

The principle of human rights, enshrined in the 1948 Universal Declaration of Human Rights, various international covenants, and the constitution of many governments, is a welcome innovation from the twentieth century. In many ways, the expansion of human rights is an entirely different field from the just war tradition, although there are a few key points of shared concern. However, there are real tensions between the two, particularly when it comes to justifications for going to war and priorities for post-conflict policy. These parallels and disjunctures will be addressed below.

Human rights did not suddenly appear in 1948. Rather, there is a long intellectual genealogy, particularly in the West, that culminated in the Universal Declaration and subsequent human rights treaties. For instance, human rights standards are informed by religious understandings of the moral worth of the individual, such as Protestant Christianity's emphasis on the individual as a moral agent. Also influential is the Enlightenment's social contract, which asserted the inherent dignity of the individual and declared that the fundamental purpose of the state was to protect and promote the life, property, and happiness of the individual, rather than the masses existing to support a few privileged elites who controlled the mechanisms of power. The influence of democratic theory in the early twentieth century—particularly President Woodrow Wilson's emphasis on self-determination and anti-colonialism—also played a role in the intellectual milieu of the Universal Declaration. Of course, the heinous crimes of the Holocaust cannot be discounted in effecting moral outrage which also contributed to the Universal Declaration and other human rights instruments.

The just war tradition played its own part in providing resources for human rights law. Just war's emphasis on *distinction* and *proportionality* was first fleshed out in international law decades before the modern human rights movement began, in covenants such as the 1868 St. Petersburg Declaration, the 1899 and 1907 Hague Conventions, and the 1925 Geneva Protocol. In each case, limitations were put on the tools of warfare (such as types of projectiles, bacteriological and chemical agents) for principled (moral outrage) and pragmatic (we do not want them used against us) reasons. Moreover, definitions were employed to distinguish the rights and protections of civilians from military personnel, such as the distinction between civilian sailors versus sailors on merchant vessels that had been converted to military service (Article VII, Hague 1907). Ultimately, within a year of the Universal Declaration, the 1949 Geneva Conventions further concretized international law rooted in these just war principles, such as explicit definitions of, and protections for, non-combatants: prisoners of war, the ship-wrecked, civilians, children, and the wounded. Thus there is a common international ethic inspiring legal admonitions of the rights and obligations of individuals and governments both in terms of human rights and on the battlefield. Of course, all of this rested on a set of historic presuppositions about the nexus of prudence and ethics in international warfare, such as notions of sovereignty and legitimate authority.

Over the past half-century, human rights have expanded in international and domestic law. The demise of the colonial system resulted in new nation-states with constitutions often modeled on those of the U.S. and France with explicit human rights guarantees for their citizens. Similarly, the aspirational Universal Declaration was fleshed out in two major treaties (and two optional protocols) which are often known collectively as the International Bill of Human Rights: The International Covenant on Civil and Political Rights (1966) and the International Covenant on Economic, Social, and Cultural Rights (1966) (with protocols). A series of related covenants followed on Torture, Racial Discrimination, Women, Children, Migrant Workers, and Persons with Disabilities.[11]

With this in mind, there are at least three similarities between just war thinking, particularly as it relates to post-conflict, and the field of human rights. The first is that sovereignty is not a moral carte blanche. A norm in international affairs that dates from at least the Peace of Westphalia (1648) is the principle of national sovereignty and the corollary of non-intervention: that legitimate national authorities have carte blanche within their borders with little fear of outside intervention. This principle has increasingly come into conflict with the notion of universal human rights and a "responsibility to protect" those suffering grave human rights abuses. There has long been an ambivalent relationship between the amoral sovereignty of international relations theory and the just war principles of *legitimate authorities* acting with *right intent* on behalf of *justice*.

It is thus clear that the other two similarities between just war thinking and human rights theory are a deep regard for justice and a concern for non-combatants. When it comes to post-conflict, a norm against violations of the immunity of non-combatants and disproportionate and immoral use of force (such as ethnic cleansing), and a positive moral principle of accountability are all shared by the two traditions. Nevertheless, there are key differences in practice, particularly when it comes to the scope and nature of justice, the issue of order and stability, and the fundamental cassus belli of war.

Just war principles—be they ad bellum, in bello, or post bellum—do differ, and sometimes conflict, when contrasted with human rights activism. One such area is the scope of the two fields: just war theory focuses on the moral content of, and therefore responsibility for, the decision to go to war and how war is fought. It is not strictly concerned with the ante bellum period except precisely as it relates to the conflict in question. The human rights tradition, in contrast, when confronted with post-conflict environments that were preceded by human rights violations—either those of the outgoing regime against its own people or of the loser (in the case of civil war or inter-state war)—is most likely to try to implement justice mechanisms that are far more expansive than dealing with the narrow question of war-time violations of the laws of armed conflict. In other words, it is one thing to take a jus post bellum approach to violations of the war convention, such as specific instances of civilian deaths or individual cases of rape, but it is a much wider scope to hold major elements of a past regime—the police, military, and senior political officials—guilty of systematic and sustained human rights violations. The latter suggests not only the probability of protracted, massive legal drama but also the possibility of destabilizing a tenuous post-conflict order.

A related difference between the just war and human rights traditions is the nature or quality of justice. Just war thinking has generally argued for restraint at war's end. For instance, Michael Walzer argues that at the end of most wars, something approximating the status quo ante bellum is preferable due to the hubris associated with hyper-expansive war aims and ideology-driven regime transformation. However, it is the common approach of the human rights community to demand radical transformative change not only in the security sector (that is, SSR) but across all the instruments of government. This transformation of the organs of government is the routine objective of the human rights community. Simply, it does not adopt the limited approach of the just war tradition, which has not historically championed a single vision of human governance.

The jus in bello principle of "discrimination" suggests that after the war, there should be some accounting for misdeeds against civilians and other violations of the war convention. Here there is some agreement between the traditions as to a moral warrant for justice. Thus, human rights law can inform the justice component of post-conflict as long as it does not erode order. Here we see a conundrum of international life: that efforts toward a more just peace can destabilize the achievement of a modest order. One wonders if the ICC indictment of Sudanese president Bashir is just such a factor, destabilizing the "interim period" following the signing of the Comprehensive Peace Agreement of 2005 between North and South Sudan, and furthermore a factor exacerbating conflict in Darfur. Perhaps it was this indictment that made rigged elections a rational choice for the regime, and fermented a return to one of the twentieth century's most bloody conflicts. Similarly, an ICC indictment may have scared off the Lord's Resistance Army's Joseph Kony from signing the Juba Accords and bringing a resolution to Uganda's two-decade-long insurgency.

A conundrum addressed in the concluding chapter has to do with competing views of the military instrument in the human rights community. On the one hand are human rights watchdogs who have spent the last generation attempting to box in that group whom they feel to be the prime enemy of human rights: national militaries. On the other hand is a sector of the human rights movement who sees armed forces as the only solution to crimes against humanity in places like Rwanda and Bosnia. These tensions, particularly in recent claims of a "responsibility to protect," are taken up in the next chapter.

In sum, just war principles such as just cause, proportionality, and discrimination foreshadowed and today have become inter-twined with human rights law. In fact, some renowned contemporary just war authors have come to argue that the only purpose of a just war is to protect or vindicate human rights. This chapter argues, in contrast, that although there are links between human rights law and jus post bellum, there remain critical distinctions between the two.

## Humanitarian Assistance

Humanitarian assistance consists of vital material and logistical assistance to save human life and mitigate suffering in situations of crisis. Its sibling—development assistance—attempts to alter or develop basic socio-economic conditions for long-term political and economic stability. There is obviously a close relationship between the mandates of these two fields, particularly because they tend to overlap in places like Afghanistan, Mozambique, and Cambodia. This chapter focuses on the assumptions and agenda of those agencies involved in humanitarian and development work during, or after, conflict (assuming some intertwining of these fields) and suggests important differences between humanitarian and just war thinking on issues of order and justice.

The activities of twenty-first-century humanitarians go well beyond just feeding the hungry; they range from international activism on issues such as landmines and small arms/light weapons proliferation, to development work, to visiting and publishing reports about the incarcerated. Thus, perhaps no one recognizes the real-world dilemmas of jus post bellum better than humanitarians, development experts, and aid workers. They work on behalf of the millions of people who exist in post- (or pre-)conflict situations that approximate Hobbes's state of war: either hot war or preparation for war "at all times." In other words, what is often called "developing" and/or "post-conflict" is in fact a "pre-conflict" situation of gross insecurity, poverty, and resentment—a smoldering powder keg ready to explode.

Interestingly, modern humanitarianism has some roots in just war concepts of proportionality and, especially, discrimination (non-combatant immunity), although the practitioner literature is almost devoid of references to the just war tradition.[12] However, there are areas where the presuppositions of humanitarians differ significantly from those of just war thinking, particularly in their views about order, justice, and neutrality. Just war theory begins with the notion that deadly force can be employed morally, with right intent and just cause, by legitimate authorities. As discussed in chapter three, this perspective is deeply rooted in Western political philosophy: the need to restrain violence on the one hand and the need to protect and punish on the other. Order is the responsibility of legitimate authority. "Legitimate" need not mean democracy, and indeed it rarely has historically. Rather, legitimate means "representative" in the most modest of senses: meeting its moral obligation to take into account the needs of its populace, particularly with regards to law and order. In short, authority is one side of the coin; fulfilling the responsibility to provide order is the other.

Much of the trauma of international life is a consequence of breakdowns in the moral political order, whether it be non-state actors threatening international security or authoritarian regimes terrorizing segments of their own populace. Weak governments (such as in Yemen and Georgia), governments that do not control their entire demarcated territory (such as in the Philippines or Colombia), or governments that harbor and/or support those who would topple other governments (such as in Sudan, Libya, or Pakistan), as well as stateless spaces (such as in Somalia, FATA, the Tri-Border Region), all suggest the tenuousness and the real-world limits of comprehensive order around the globe. The hungry families living in gross insecurity in such places experience the effects of weak institutions and disorder in their struggle to survive.

Humanitarians see all of these conditions and act to alleviate human suffering, regardless of regime type or long-term political orientation. Their work is responsible for the basic survival of tens of millions of people every year in some of the direst conditions imaginable: war, famine, disease, natural disaster. Their philosophical orientation is pragmatic and victim-focused in the field, with little grand-theorizing about political order and regime type. For example, the mission statement of one of the premiere non-profit organizations involved in post-conflict landmine and explosive ordnance removal is simply, "Getting Mines Out of the Ground, Now."[13] The mission statement of the International Committee of the Red Cross declares an "exclusively humanitarian mission is to protect the lives and dignity of victims of armed conflict and other situations of violence and to provide them with assistance." Both of these organizations exemplify hundreds of others in their mission, commitments, and their claims of neutrality. The former, for example, declares in the preamble to its mission statement, that it is "non-political and non-religious"; the ICRC similarly is an "impartial, neutral and independent organization."

Humanitarian agencies have a keen sense that violence is generally wrong. This often pits their activism, in a general sense, against national militaries—regardless of regime type. Hence, many political leaders and their general officers (focused on order and national security), whether in a democracy or an authoritarian regime, may find themselves in opposition to humanitarian agencies when it comes to the international politics of specific weapons systems, refugee flows, access to prisoners (terrorists), defense spending, and the like. Over the past quarter-century many humanitarian and development agencies, like the ICRC and Oxfam, have been increasingly vocal at the UN and other international fora. A case in point was a white paper published by Oxfam and six other humanitarian organizations during the January 2010 Afghanistan donors' conference held in London. The white paper castigated the "militarization" of humanitarian assistance in Afghanistan.[14] This demonstrates the differing perspectives of humanitarians and [some] national governments on how to create and support a durable political and economic order.

A critical difference between the just war tradition and the humanitarian field concerns the notion of neutrality. Marion Harroff-Tavel of the International Committee of the Red Cross argues that humanitarians must operate within a framework of neutrality. She explicitly asserts that the just war tradition, with its notions of right, wrong, and guilty parties is inappropriate for humanitarians, although she acknowledges how frustrating a position of neutrality is to most soldiers and national leaders.[15]

Why neutrality? Why is it that humanitarian groups usually do not direct their moral outrage at the antagonists in the conflict, even when one (or more) sides are particularly egregious violators of local and international law? It is understandable, in part, if the humanitarian organization sees its role as providing succor to the very weakest; it is likely that a base level of relationship with the offensive regime (or multiple competing sides in a civil war) is necessary to get "behind enemy lines" to feed and aid those desperately in need, such as in refugee camps.

Humanitarian pledges of neutrality—to help anyone in need in a conflict or post-conflict environment—make them unwilling to make moral judgments about legitimacy and morality of rogue or oppressive regimes. Indeed, a problem commonly raised in the literature is that humanitarian actors can actually bolster failing or rogue regimes, such as by feeding the populace and thereby allowing the regime to direct resources to armaments.[16] In short, humanitarians view moral agency in terms of their "calling" to help those in need, with no judgment made about politics, justice, or the morality of the belligerents.

In contrast jus post bellum, as elucidated in this book, is deeply concerned with moral distinctions and issues of justice. For centuries, just war has made the distinction between combatants and noncombatants not merely a legal, but importantly, a moral imperative. Just war thinking considers the obligation of political authorities to provide security, prevent conflict, and punish wrongdoing to be a moral obligation—and the basis for enduring peace. Furthermore, jus post bellum's focus on justice in post-conflict situations is an important pillar to transcending the past and transforming the present in pursuit of long-term stability, and thus is qualitatively different from the core commitments of most humanitarian organizations.

In conclusion, it is true that just war thinking and humanitarians are separated by major differences of ideas and identity. This does not make them opposed, nor does it make them enemies—it makes the two fields different. The realities of contemporary post-conflict mean that humanitarians, aid experts, diplomats, and soldiers are all working "cheek by jowl" in insecure settings with shared goals of ending human suffering and advancing peace. At times their core commitments, such as neutrality vs. justice, may be in conflict, but obviously there are synergies, or better, divisions of labor, that can help establish a stable post-conflict environment and make a renewal of conflict less likely. For example, without a durable socio-political order at war's end, from basic safety to confidence that the land can be tilled and that the water can be drawn safely, anything more than basic humanitarian support is unlikely to be achieved.

## International Law/Organizations

International law is typically divided into customary law and treaty-based law. The former is rooted in the common practices of states over the centuries, the latter—as its name implies—derives from formal agreements among governments. Both types of international law have long been influenced by the just war tradition. For example, the customs of state sovereignty are historically rooted in the just war doctrine of legitimate authority; sovereignty's corollary of non-intervention is based in just war thinking's objective of restraining the cassus belli as well as limiting the destructiveness of war. In parallel, states have signed international covenants that have fleshed out the jus in bello principles of proportionality and discrimination, such as in The Hague and Geneva Conventions and the International Torture Convention. These binding international laws represent one facet of what Michael Walzer calls the "triumph of just war theory."[17]

A third, or better related, type of agreement that states make in international affairs is to give life to an international organization. This is usually done to promote mutual interests, such as collective security (such as the League of Nations) or economic rationalization (such as the World Trade Organization). When it comes to issues of war and peace, the UN Charter—written in the shadow of World War II's horrors—represents a further attempt to implement prudential and moral limits on warfare, such as designating it the province only of legitimate state actors and attempting to limit the situations in which the resort to force is justified, namely self-defense. The Charter suggests a collective global responsibility for peace and security ("collective security") among sovereign powers and recognizes a variety of associated obligations of governments, such as the security and prosperity of their citizens as well as those persons under their control (such as colonies). According to the Charter's logic, essentially any inter-state war is unjustified (on one or both sides) because aggression is always unjustified. The Charter asserts that it is up to the Security Council to authorize any use of force other than in self-defense of a government (meaning any unauthorized armed outside intervention is illegitimate).

In short, over the past century just war principles have been formalized as the laws of armed conflict and they reside within the core DNA of international organizations. This is true of the UN as well as NATO, the African Union, and other regional associations. What does this portend for just war thinking? Are there conflicts between just war thinking and international law/organizations? And what specifically of jus post bellum? A number of observations are in order about the tensions between legality and morality, legalism and prudence, and the role and perspective of international organizations like the UN.

First, an obvious difference between international law and just war thinking is that the former is binary: something is legal or it is illegal. This can paint the world in black and white, and, at least in theory, means that all decisions about war and peace are actually quite easy: either it is legal or it is not. In contrast, from the perspective of just war thinking, there may be significant differences between legality and morality. Although it can be useful to have simple, black-and-white standards about who can legitimately go to war under defined circumstances, due to the institutional mechanics of organizations like the UN, what is moral may technically be illegal. Consider the intervention that averted a Balkan bloodbath in Kosovo as discussed in chapter three. In 1999 the UN Security Council refused to authorize force in the region despite the fact that all signs indicated ethnic cleansing was once again underway in the former Yugoslavia. At the time, Serbia was still led by war criminal President Slobodan Milošević, who in 1990 began a decade-long policy of repression in Kosovo. The Security Council avoided approving intervention to stop the violence, largely due to a Russian veto.

NATO responded to the crisis with a seventy-eight-day Allied aerial coercion campaign that not only ended Serbian aggression, but in the long run contributed to regional security in neighboring Macedonia and Albania. A decade later, Kosovo followed a UN-sanctioned path to statehood and is now recognized by over sixty other countries. That decade, as described earlier in this book, exemplified jus post bellum in the sense of the obligation that the intervening powers felt toward real stability in the region—spending billions of dollars on reconstructing a Kosovar state. Despite all this, many international legal theorists continue to see the Kosovo intervention and "occupation" as illegal, even though it was clearly the moral policy alternative. The potential ramifications for engagement in places such as Burma and Sudan are significant.

A second distinction between just war thinking and international law is in the area of prudence, such as in decisions about employing force (jus ad bellum), decisions about how force is employed (jus in bello), and decisions about post-conflict arrangements (jus post bellum). It is entirely possible for international law to authorize, or disallow, unwise or imprudent courses of action. One example of this is the Convention on the Prohibition of the Use, Stockpiling, Production and Transfer of Anti-Personnel Mines and on Their Destruction, otherwise known as the Ottawa Treaty or the Mine Ban Treaty.[18] Signed on December 3, 1997, and taking effect two years later, the Ottawa Treaty today has over 150 signatories. The treaty specifically bans all use of anti-personnel landmines (though not anti-tank mines and associated munitions), commits countries to destroy their arsenals of anti-personnel landmines within four years of signing the treaty (with an exception of a small cache of mines for mine and explosive ordnance removal training), prohibits all future manufacture of anti-personnel landmines, and commits members to the complete and total removal of minefields within their own territories.

How does prudential jus post bellum apply? Landmines are a terrible scourge that remain active long after the hot phase of a war ends; it would seem that a lawful ban on them would be appropriate. It has been well documented, however, that poor countries who sign on to the Ottawa Treaty commit themselves to immediate, expensive action to remove all landmines in their soil—even if those mines are in remote locations that pose no danger to civilians, such as in remote Egyptian deserts (a legacy of World War II) or inaccessible mountain passes in the Falkland Islands. One has to wonder at the prudential cost-benefit analysis of some of these activities in less economically developed countries.

However, such examples—even if seeming unwise and doctrinaire from a policy standpoint—do not necessarily pose an insoluble case for jus post bellum concepts of order and justice. What of the case where the deterrent threat posed by landmines contributes to security in the post-conflict situation, such as to delimit a controversial border? Their use then is clearly prudential, and perhaps even moral. The demilitarized zone between the Koreas is a case in point. I have written elsewhere about how the armistice that postponed further hostilities in the Korean Conflict ended the hot phase of a war that cost one million casualties per year over a four-year period.[19] That war never ended with a comprehensive peace agreement; instead, hostilities were suspended under the armistice of 1953. That truce has held for nearly sixty years, despite numerous difficult moments, including in 2010 the sinking of a South Korean vessel by a North Korean torpedo.

Although it is a bitterly cold peace, nonetheless, most years no one dies in inter-state conflict on the Korean Peninsula. What have kept the peace are the robust security measures on either side, including a heavily mined demilitarized zone (DMZ). On the South Korean side, the "Korean Security Barrier" (KSB) consists of minefields, fences, concertina wire, and the like—an important safeguard against North Korean invasion aimed at Seoul (just 27 miles south of the DMZ). As an article in the *Journal of Mine Action* states, "Landmines used by responsible governments in monitored military situations are an effective method of achieving peace without producing casualties to non-combatants."[20]

The point about jus post bellum is clear: the primary post-conflict goal must be security, and leaders must have the pragmatic sensibilities to think through the best course of action for founding an enduring peace. However, the letter of the law in this instance is that, should the U.S. and its allies join the Ottawa Treaty (and there is tremendous pressure to do so), then the minefields of the DMZ would have to be dismantled. Clearly, a black-and-white interpretation of the law in this case would be destabilizing and unwise, potentially contributing to future conflict.

A third area of potential friction is between just war thinking and the approach of international institutions, most notably the UN. Elsewhere I have articulated many of the challenges that supranational institutions such as the UN face when it comes to thinking and acting ethically in times of conflict. For instance, when states fail and other states intervene via supranational agencies, who is morally responsible? When states fail and their neighbors refuse to intervene, who is morally responsible? And finally, when states turn to international agencies, notably the UN, NATO, or the African Union (AU) to act where individual states have refused to act, who is morally responsible? The cases of Bosnia, Somalia, and Rwanda come to mind.

The UN answer regarding legitimacy and authority is that votes of the Security Council confer legality on its actions with regard to conflict. Nonetheless, issues of moral agency and accountability, from blue helmets raping civilians in West Africa to the billions of dollars lost (and civilians deprived of basic necessities) due to the Iraq Oil-for-Food scam—which implicated the son of the UN Secretary General—should make us pause when considering issues of order, justice, and conciliation under the auspices of international organizations.

Just war by committee is likely to achieve little that is just or effective in fighting wars, punishing evil-doers, and halting aggression. Indeed, a problem shared by the EU, the African Union, and the UN is the tendency to inaction when action is called for. The hallmark of such collectives is dithering when responsible action is required. Why is this the case? Supranational organizations, especially the UN, tend to require consensus among members to act. Because the UN is not a unified whole with a single set of interests, it is often paralyzed because its constituents cannot agree on action. This is certainly the case for any of the murderous wars of the 1990s in Europe, Asia, and Africa.

If military humanitarian intervention did finally occur in such cases, it was generally undermanned and poorly supported, as exemplified by UN inaction in Congo and AU impotence in Darfur. Furthermore, when it comes to conflict, international organizations tend to approach conflict in mutually destabilizing ways. If international forces are on the ground and contribute to bringing the conflict to an end (a rare occurrence), then their governments want them to redeploy home as soon as possible—despite the conditions of insecurity on the ground. At the same time, the international community tends to pour millions of dollars of development monies into such environments, as if more money is the solution. The fact is that floods of cash into insecure post-conflict scenarios increase the likelihood of corruption and violent competition for resources.

Finally, how does all of this relate to jus post bellum? Ending wars well is about a moral and political commitment to order, long-term goals of peace, security, justice, and conciliation. International laws and organizations simply do not have the resources to make this happen, nor can international organizations ever substitute for the pre-conditions of an enduring, local peace. Fundamentally, the essential difference between the prudential ethics of just war thinking and the legalist paradigm of international law and organizations is contrasting views of order: the former in terms of legitimate authorities meeting their moral obligations in political life, the latter defining order in terms of a web of formal agreements and the aspiration that such agreements will be fulfilled.

## Conclusion

This chapter began with the premise that in recent years a number of sub-disciplines or fields have developed that have some bearing on late- and post-conflict situations, as well as in that murky phase where "post-" and "pre-conflict" intersect, such as the Rwandan interregnum of 1992–1994. This chapter evaluated the relationship of jus post bellum to these other fields, describing linkages, connections, and critical distinctions. It will have been successful if it sparks debate and research across multiple disciplines.

To be clear, jus post bellum is not an amalgam of these approaches. It is simply not true that we can bundle any and all good ideas about post-conflict into an omnibus approach to ending wars well that is consonant with the just war tradition. As demonstrated above, key differences emerge between the fields in theory and in practice, whether it be about the power realities of post-conflict, misunderstanding different levels of analysis, normative trade-offs between order, justice, and reconciliation, moral agency, or the limits of the discipline (such as beyond war to political transitions).

The comparisons demonstrate the utility and suggest some boundaries of a just war approach to ending wars well. A coherent, just war theory–inspired approach to late- and post-conflict will limit itself to war, from its causes to its conclusion. It will restrain itself from awkwardly trying to chime in other domains, allowing other disciplines to do their own work. Yet when just war scholarship remains true to its historic fundamentals of order, restraint, and justice it continues to be a vital, dynamic approach for considering the ethics of conflict and post-conflict in a changing world.

## CHAPTER 7

# 21st-Century Challenges
## *R2P, Stability Ops, Afghanistan, and Beyond*

War is paradoxical. It can be the scene of some of humanity's worst suffering—as seen in East Timor, Kosovo, Afghanistan, and Sudan in recent years. It can also be the setting for individual acts of valor, of courageous choices, and of historic statesmanship. War can also be decisive—it can set in motion a process that destabilizes entire regions for decades, or, alternately, it can result in a reordering of political realities that is stable and enduring.

There is no magic formula for ending wars well. That being said, just war thinking offers interrelated principles for post-conflict peace: Order, Justice, and Conciliation. To be clear, this is not a grand theory but a framework, an outline informed by the just war tradition that must be fleshed out on a case-by-case basis: pay the price for real Order, work for Justice when practicable, and consider some form of Conciliation if possible . . . all without eroding the Order.

In sum, all wars that end well establish a secure Order, and in some cases implement ensuing mechanisms for Justice and Conciliation that can broaden and deepen the peace. Figure 1 portrays this graphically: that Order is the foundation for enduring peace, that the three principles overlap and influence one another, and that cases of satisfying Justice and Conciliation are few.

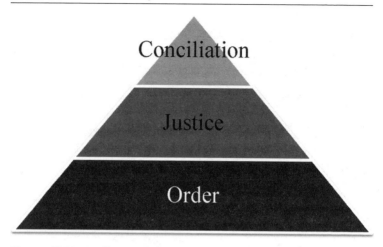

Figure 1: Elements of *jus post bellum*.

Just getting to Order can be a herculean ordeal. Order is most likely to occur when one side convincingly defeats its adversary on the battlefield, as the Union battered the Confederacy, the Entente defeated the Triple Alliance in 1918, and the Allies crushed the Nazis and Imperial Japan in 1945. More recently, we have seen decisive victories by the RPF in Rwanda (1994) and by the Sri Lankan government (2009). Decisive victory allows a window for uncontested elimination of threats to security and establishment of the basics of political order. History testifies to how costly and difficult such victories can be to win, as in each of these cases, but they do provide an opportunity to found a secure post-conflict order.

It is even more expensive to win outright victory and then fail to establish the peace. Victors have an obligation to practice restraint, yet impose Order—admittedly a difficult balance—as Rwanda experienced in 1994–1998. It is not difficult to squander the moment of victory and thus lose the peace, as occurred in Iraq in 2003. More recently, Sri Lanka's government won a twenty-five-year-long civil war against the Tamil Tigers in 2009, but seems determined to throw away the momentum for lasting peace through factional infighting, poor post-conflict planning, disregard for the adversary's survivors, and an unwillingness to pursue justice or national reconciliation. In short, Sri Lanka seems determined to cripple the Order it achieved after a quarter-century of bloodshed.

The fundamental responsibility of political actors, in war or peace, is to work toward Order. In post-conflict settings, Order begins with stopping the killing and the exercise of sovereignty by a single point of authority. Order extends its roots through the maturation of government capacity and services. As outlined in chapter three, there are military (traditional security), governance (domestic politics), and international security conditions to a basic post-conflict order that must be met and extended if there is to be lasting peace.

The military dimension regards the definitive termination of "hot" conflict, with the tools of warfare resting solely in the hands of legitimate authorities. This means that all belligerents have agreed to the cessation of conflict; there are no organized, armed spoilers or insurgents lurking in the countryside to destabilize the peace deal. All parties must support the new security arrangement by no longer challenging it via military force. Military considerations of Order also begin to take account of the appropriate structuring of military strength and forces to sustain a robust defense without undermining the security of formal rivals.

All of these efforts to confirm military aspects of post-conflict Order should work in tandem with domestic and international political objectives while being careful to buttress, rather than erode, the basic peace settlement. Hence, the governance dimension of Order is imposition and maintenance of the domestic rule of law. It implies a national political entity which exercises sovereignty over the legitimate use of force at home, as well as political sovereignty over its policies at home and in relations with its neighbors. However, in some cases the resumption of sovereignty follows a period of political rehabilitation, whether in the aftermath of military defeat (post–World War II Japan) or political tutelage and reconstruction (East Timor). In either case, Order means focusing on the fundamental tasks of governance, including over the economic sector.

The third dimension of Order is the international security dimension, which means that the state no longer faces an imminent threat from an internal or external foe nor is the country a threat to the peace and security of its neighbors (such as refugee flows). The international security dimension is intertwined with and reinforces both basic internal security and efforts at governance. In sum, the very first steps toward a longer-term, more robust domestic and national situation of security begin with the grueling task of implementing Order in these three dimensions.

In short, to end well all wars must establish Order—whether or not there is an avenue for Justice. But in some cases, an approximation of Justice is possible and appropriate. However obvious this sounds, the actual application of "just deserts" is extremely difficult in practice. The most promising venue for justice is at home—the prosecution of violations of the war convention by one's own soldiers. The U.S., for example, has punished its own in recent years, including prison terms, fines, dishonorable discharges, and hard labor for the guards at Abu Ghraib. Another form of justice is the punishment of those elites responsible for planning and implementing aggressive policies, such as Napoleon's exile to St. Helena or the execution of Saddam Hussein. Punishment restrains those actors from further aggression, punishes them for their misdeeds, and avenges the victims.

Punishment is Justice focused on the crimes of aggressors, but there is another side to Justice that focuses on victims: restitution. Restitution attempts to acknowledge that wrong was done and compensate victims for their losses. In practice, though, reparations tend to be paid as government-to-government indemnities rather than amends to individual citizens, and in many cases—such as post–World War I Germany or Iraq in the 1990s—draconian reparations have been used as a bludgeon to punish perpetrators in a way that is destabilizing. Hence, restitution in post-conflict, like punishment, is an applied principle of Justice that must be considered carefully on a case-by-case basis.

The third element of the jus post bellum framework is Conciliation. Admittedly, real efforts at national and international conciliation are rare. This is due, in part, to the misperception that the path to peace and security begins with justice and reconciliation. It does not. Order must precede Conciliation, but—and this is a critical point—Order and Conciliation can be intertwined and reinforcing. In the few cases of international Conciliation, acts of conciliation occurred well after the hot conflict and followed from changes in the strategic interests of former belligerents. The rapprochement of France and Germany, occasioned by Allied occupation and the Soviet threat, ultimately led over time to the conciliatory policies of German chancellor Willy Brandt in 1970–1972.

In cases of civil war, a model of Conciliation based on changing interests, an evolving security situation, and some sort of political "forgiveness" policy (such as amnesty) may reinforce Order, ameliorate Justice claims, and transcend the status quo security dilemma. This is the sort of peace that is desirable, but it is extremely rare. As reported in chapter four, one study found less than a dozen real attempts at political forgiveness and national reconciliation in civil conflicts out of hundreds of possible cases since World War II. Of those, a third failed.

Is the Order-Justice-Conciliation framework truly consistent with traditional just war thinking? Does this model for jus post bellum comport with the presuppositions of jus ad bellum and jus in bello? Yes. The just war tradition begins with the presupposition that warfare occurs within a moral universe—however fragile and tragic—and thus just war promotes restraint in both the justification for going to war and in the tactics employed in warfighting. The early formulations of just war theory, such as by Augustine, argued that it was the duty of political authorities to protect the vulnerable, deter aggression, punish wrongdoers, and right wrongs. In classical just war language, *legitimate authorities* were responsible to act with *right intent* and *just cause* in fulfilling their obligations to the moral, and political, order. These jus ad bellum principles inform this book's argument about the primacy of political order, the critical role of political and social elites, and the ethics of Order and Justice. Pragmatic jus ad bellum principles, most notably likelihood of success, also inform the arguments in chapters three through five about the tensions between Order, Justice, and Conciliation and the necessity of political prudence in implementing post-conflict settlements, lest vindictive forms of justice or utopian visions of reconciliation undermine the success of the fragile post-conflict order.

Furthermore, the jus in bello tenets of discrimination and proportionality are inherent to the book's basic approach, particularly to Justice and Conciliation. A conflict settlement and post-war political order that seeks justice must be able to discriminate between the guilty (such as aggressive national leaders, violators of the war convention) and the innocent, between combatants and non-combatants, between war criminals and petty criminals. Attempts at justice must be proportionate to the wrongs incurred and must be implemented in ways that are restrained, lest they destabilize the tenuous post-conflict Order.

Finally, for Conciliation to develop roots and mature, it must include major political actors (legitimate authorities), not just wishful peacemaking activists, and it must acknowledge issues of security, difference, and justice associated with the conflict. What would be most desirable is a secure post-conflict scenario where all feel that Justice has been satisfied and where factions and nations are reconciled and living in harmony. Frankly, such is not realistic for many reasons. However, considering the world as it actually is need not lead us to despair: it must focus our attention as scholars, warriors, diplomats, and policymakers on avenues for successful and creative policy in the twenty-first century.

In a 2010 lecture at Georgetown University, Michael Walzer pointed to a number of the just war issues attendant in contemporary post-conflicts, particularly those that the U.S. and its allies find themselves engaged in, notably Iraq, Afghanistan, and developing world-humanitarian interventions.[1] A brief look at the issues Walzer addressed links the previous chapters to the final section of this book: a look at how contemporary post-conflict doctrine at the UN and in the U.S. attempts to operationalize policies for late- and post-conflict scenarios.

Walzer argues that the immediate post-conflict environment requires *provision* (meeting the survival needs of human beings) and *reconstruction* (infrastructure, homes, livelihoods). In conflicts like Iraq and Afghanistan, the Coalition has a responsibility to provide for the populace as it is the arguably victorious intervening power, which bases its claim to legitimacy on helping non-combatants be free from tyranny. Provision and reconstruction are critical dimensions of the post-conflict order; otherwise, the populace will starve and the region will be prey to internal and external security challenges. Nonetheless, from the perspectives of policy and ethics, a number of issues immediately come to the fore. First, *who* has an obligation to do *what?* Some form of political authority assumes an obligation to provide for the post-conflict order, from law enforcement to provision for the survival needs of the populace to protecting the borders. But how far does that obligation extend in practice? Providing potable water? Combating disease? Pensions for military veterans? Pensions for senior citizens? University education?

The "what" is challenging to define without getting at the "who." Obligation implies relationship—there is a benefactor and a beneficiary. How do these relationships form in contemporary post-conflict? The issue is further problematized, as Walzer suggests, because many of the contemporary wars that the West has engaged in are armed humanitarian interventions rather than classical conflicts between state governments. In classic warfare, the roles of the protagonists were clear and there was little sense of moral obligation at war's end.

In contrast, for much of the past quarter-century the West has chosen a different post-conflict approach, one where there is not a winner and a loser, victor and vanquished, but rather aggressors, victims, and the international community. The Balkan wars of the 1990s are cases in point: aggressor Serbs, victimized Bosnian Muslims, and the international community to the rescue. The international community (that is, NATO) did not claim the mantle of "victor" in Bosnia or Kosovo, but neither did it absorb the loser or simply go home. Instead, following a precedent set after World War II but neglected for much of the Cold War, the intervening powers—at great expense to themselves and with little sense of vital interests—chose to not only provide provision and reconstruction, but provided billions in an attempt to transform Bosnia and Kosovo into capitalist democracies, as well as East Timor, Afghanistan, and a half dozen other cases. Walzer asked the audience to reconsider the notion of *trusteeship*, which has negative associations due to colonialism and the "mandate" system in the Middle East during the early twentieth century. Trusteeship may lead to political transformation.

All of this suggests that we need more scholarly and policy attention to whether or not there actually are ethical obligations to provision, reconstruction, and transformation; to the nature of the moral agents involved; and to the ethical obligations of winners, losers, aggressors, victims, and especially interveners. Walzer particularly noted the oxymoron of humanitarian intervention: governments who do not intervene take on no responsibility (such as the Chinese); those who make a "citizen's arrest" and intervene take on obligation for ending the conflict and for its aftermath—the proverbial "no good deed goes unpunished."

This suggests an order issue that Walzer calls the *ethics of exit:* when should the victorious intervening power leave and allow domestic institutions full autonomy over their affairs? When is enough, enough? Obviously, *provision, reconstruction, transformation,* and *exit* are primarily order issues but also inextricably linked to deeper philosophical issues about security, justice, and (re)conciliation. It is the operationalization of these issues in policy and practice to which we turn.

## New Government Doctrine on Post-Conflict: Jus Post Bellum or Nation-Building?

As acknowledged in chapter two, over the past five years some scholars have begun to consider the unfinished business of just war theory: its application to late- and post-conflict. In that same time period there has been more post-conflict thinking done by government actors than in the entire previous century. With the early disappointments of Afghanistan and Iraq in mind, as well as the frustrations of recurrent conflict in the 1990s, government bodies have developed operational frameworks for dealing with post-conflict, such as the International Commission on Intervention and State Sovereignty's (ICISS) Responsibility to Protect document, the U.S. State Department's Post-Conflict Essential Tasks, and the U.S. Army's Field Manual for Stabilization Operations. Each of these documents and the agencies they represent highlight some of the key points of this book while overlooking and extending others.

## R2P AND THE RESPONSIBILITY TO REBUILD

The Responsibility to Protect document derived from a Canadian-sponsored initiative, ICISS, to galvanize international support for a robust intervention mandate in grotesque cases of human suffering. Canada is keenly aware of this issue: it was a Canadian general who oversaw the failed UN mission in Rwanda during the 1994 genocide. The R2P document asserts more than just a moral responsibility to intervene on behalf of human life: it declares a "responsibility to rebuild in the three most immediately crucial areas of security, justice and economic development." That responsibility begins with "basic security and protection for all members of a population" and extends through demobilizaiton, disarmament, and reintegration (DDR), the development of adequate police and national military units, and the reconstruction of a national judiciary and national law in the service of individual rights (such as property) and economic development. To summarize, the "responsibility to rebuild" is to impose security, install juridical and law enforcement mechanisms, and deeply invest in economic development.

At first glance, this ICISS's "responsibility to rebuild" sounds akin to this book's approach to jus post bellum. In part, this is due to R2P's rehearsal of just war tenets (proportionality, discrimination) and its emphasis on decisively stopping the killing and basic security. Nonetheless, the "responsibility to rebuild" says nothing about the deeper context-specific philosophical questions as to the nature of political order and the implementation of post-conflict justice. Strangely, it calls only for the apprehension of intervening troops who violate the laws of armed conflict, remaining mute on punishing those who initiated the conflict or locals who violated the war convention. On domestic justice it offers the following cookie-cutter approach: "A number of non-governmental bodies have developed 'justice packages,' which can be adapted to the specific conditions of a wide variety of operations."[2] In short, the "responsibility to rebuild" puts zero responsibility on the host nation while imposing huge obligations on interveners, assuming that a "package" of Western institutions and monies will somehow make everything turn out all right. The document concludes, "True and lasting reconciliation occurs with sustained daily efforts at repairing infrastructure, at rebuilding housing, at planting and harvesting, and cooperating in other productive activities."[3] Hence, whereas R2P begins with a noble aspiration, to save human life, the "responsibility to rebuild" shows its true colors—it is a grand scheme for nation-building, financial transfers from Western donors, and political transformation. It is not, on paper at least, characterized by the just war presupposition of restraint.

Individual Western governments have developed their own approaches to post-conflict, usually in the form of "stabilization operations" doctrine worked out while watching the security indices of Afghanistan and Iraq disintegrate. Indeed, most of these agencies were founded within one year of each other in 2005, such as Canada's Stabilization and Reconstruction Task Force (START), the U.S. State Department's Office of the Coordinator for Reconstruction and Stabilization (S/CRS), and the U.K.'s interagency Stabilisation Unit. The British Government defines "stabilisation" as "the process of establishing peace and security in countries affected by conflict and instability . . . the promotion of peaceful political settlement to produce a legitimate indigenous government, which can better serve its people."[4]

The U.S. began to extend its thinking on post-conflict after three tough years in Afghanistan and more than a year in Iraq. On December 7, 2004, President George W. Bush signed National

Security Presidential Directive 44 (NSPD-44), which gave the Department of State the lead role in coordinating interagency efforts at post-conflict management through a new office, the Coordinator for Reconstruction and Stability Operations. Before 2004 there had been no such focal point, nor had the U.S. engaged in operations of this magnitude in recent memory, although for decades the U.S. military had doctrine on what many call "Phase 4 Operations." By 2005 the State Department had issued a 54-page document outlining the "Post-Conflict Reconstruction Essential Tasks."[5] The Defense Department responded to NSPD-44 with DoD Directive 3000.05, which defined "stability operations" as a "core military mission . . . to maintain or reestablish a safe and secure environment, provide essential government services, emergency infrastructure reconstruction, and humanitarian relief."[6] Furthermore, the U.S. military is directed to "assist other U.S. Government agencies, foreign governments and security forces, and government organizations in . . . reconstruction and stabilization efforts, to include:" DDR, creating "legitimate security forces," "strengthening governance and the rule of law," and "fostering economic stability and development." Within a few years, the U.S. internalized this directive and the changed strategic environment with an updated version of its Field Manual for "Stability Operations" (FM 3–07). USAID followed suit with a series of post-conflict "toolkits" for practitioners working in unstable environments.[7]

These documents, written while the Iraq and Afghanistan conflicts were unfolding, rightly prioritize security. FM 3–07 discusses how the military can work with other U.S. government and outside partners to "leverage the coercive and constructive capabilities of the military force to establish a safe and secure environment; facilitate reconciliation among local or regional adversaries; establish political, legal, social, and economic institutions; and facilitate the transition of responsibility to a legitimate civil authority."[8] FM 3–07 explicitly links to the State Department's five "stability sectors": security, justice and reconciliation, humanitarian assistance and social well-being, governance and participation, and economic stabilization and infrastructure.

From a historical point of view, the flood of these new offices, agencies, and documents indicates a tipping point in awareness about post-conflict and the interests of the U.S. and allied governments. In terms of themes, these documents talk a great deal about the importance of "security," "justice," and "reconciliation." The manuals provide an encyclopedic compendium of activities in each of the five stability sectors that can help a country move from establishing a safe and secure environment to consolidation of a twenty-first-century liberal democracy, from ceasefire to "creat[ing] conditions conducive to formation of stock and commodity markets"; all in just a few dozen pages. They are important advances in operationalizing the concepts of Order, Justice, and Conciliation.

What these documents do not do, however, is discuss any of the trade-offs inherent in efforts at national security and political order on the one hand, and issues of justice and (re)conciliation on the other. Furthermore, as is the case for R2P, the reader can identify normative presuppositions (such as transparency and anti-corruption, legal system reform, civil society freedoms, social safety net), but there is no discussion whatever about how these values are embedded in a Western, liberal worldview and therefore are likely to induce debate—if not outright conflict—over many such issues in Southern and Eastern societies.

These issues do not negate the utility of these documents, but they raise the issue of the contextual nature of Order, Justice, and Conciliation in post-conflict. It is one thing to stop the bullets; it is another thing altogether to reassemble a playbook from El Salvador in Somalia or Afghanistan. Moreover, the just war tradition of restraint and its attendant concern for the hubris which inspires ever-inflating war aims should give one pause, lest the pursuit of noble causes become a crusade. In short, these documents describe far more than a modest post-conflict peace: any document that soberly outlines how outsiders can transform a society from mass violence to public works to a national stock exchange in just a few pages is describing a revolution.

## Jus Post Bellum and Afghanistan

Iraq (2003) was a case of missed opportunities—the Coalition won the war and lost, for a time, the peace. Afghanistan, however, is different. Afghanistan is a security will-of-the-wisp, and therefore it presents a novel challenge to the argument of this book. Security, Stability, Order. The ways these concepts are conceived in the West is alien to many in Afghanistan, and therefore the Afghan case (since 2001) has been a civilizational challenge not to the U.S. military and its allies, but to foundational Western ideas about the rightly ordered society and justice. Afghanistan is a critical case for jus post bellum: does it refute the model? The answer is "no." Afghanistan is not a repudiation of the framework, but it should force a recalibration of thinking about how to employ Order, Justice, and Conciliation in harsh environments.

The fundamental dilemma in Afghanistan is the multidimensionality of Order. On the one hand, the mission of the October–November 2001 U.S./NATO invasion was to punish Osama bin Laden and his organization, and thereby remove a threat to international security. Al Qaeda and its Taliban allies were defeated—or more accurately, fled to the hills—after just ninety days of war; but it was not a complete victory because they never surrendered or were destroyed. Local insecurity continued while the West implemented the sort of post-conflict cookie-cutter "packages" envisaged by the R2P document. The stated goal was rehabilitation of the Afghan polity; the real objective—when one looks at the London and Tokyo donor conferences—was nothing short of massive, deep-seated transformation of Afghan society. In other words, from early on the war aims shifted from "deter, defeat, and destroy" terrorists to nation-building.

The nation-building program combined efforts to promote security and political reform with economic development. Afghanistan's UN-managed DDR program, titled the "Afghan New Beginnings Program,"[9] demobilized over 62,000 former combatants and provided assistance to them and an additional 11,000 children and 25,000 women at a cost of $100 million.[10] This combined with massive efforts to create and/or reform Afghanistan's law enforcement, courts, departments of government, military, and every other aspect of the state. Furthermore, an Afghan Independent Human Rights Commission (AIHRC) was created, which adopted an Action Plan on Peace, Reconciliation, and Justice in December 2005 that called for formal remembrance of victims, human rights vetting of government officials and truth-seeking.[11] Through it all, donors were convinced that lack of economic development was a "root cause" of disorder, and hence billions of dollars were invested in Afghanistan's economic development.

The inability to obliterate the Taliban and al Qaeda was not just a military affair—it portended a far deeper, much more elusive war of ideas between competing conceptions of a rightly ordered society.[12] To this day, tens of thousands, if not millions, of Afghans—especially Pashtuns—maintain conceptions of Order and Justice that are rooted in local cultural norms (such as the honor code of *pashtunwaliya*), kinship networks, patriarchal lines of authority, and traditional forms of Islam. The arduous task of the Karzai government and its Western benefactors has been to establish a Western political order radiating from Kabul in a regional environment of competing concepts of legitimacy, authority, and justice. In sum, not only has basic security been difficult to establish, but there is also no shared conception of Order among the citizenry. Neither side has been able to completely defeat its opponent, thus allowing a war of ideas over competing models of Order to destabilize the country.

Afghanistan is more than a challenge to modern, Western-inspired notions of political Order: it also reveals dilemmas for Justice. The original U.S./NATO goal was punishment of Osama bin Laden and his associates, "dead or alive," and thus deterrence of future terrorist attacks by al Qaeda. One can only wonder how history might have been different had Mullah Omar handed over bin Laden and his accomplices to face justice in September 2001. Over time though, the Justice issues in this conflict have become complicated and overlapping. No longer is there a sole Justice claim against murderous terrorists. After a decade of war comprehensive Justice must take into account additional factors: local compensation for "collateral damage" by Western militaries, the impunity with which the Taliban continues to violate national law, and the hypocrisy and corruption endemic to regional warlords and the Government of Afghanistan at the national and provincial levels.

All of this violence, corruption, and injustice point to how the basic principles of fairness and "just deserts" can undermine the very foundations of Order. Afghan citizens rightfully question whether they are incurring what they deserve when caught in the crossfire, and whether the actions of the Government of Afghanistan, NATO, and the U.S. are being held to some standard of Justice. Pakistani citizens, fearing not only the Taliban and drone attacks but a corrupt and ineffectual government, are likewise deeply concerned about Order and Justice. In short, when Justice is perverted and corrupted, it attacks the roots of Order.

Finally, what of Conciliation? Early on, the international community and the Transitional Government of Afghanistan put into practice a series of conciliatory programs, such as DDR, a national *loya jirga* or consultative assembly of Afghan elites, and a human rights commission to promote a new culture of human rights accountability, particularly on behalf of women. Since 2009 there has been much talk about some form of grand bargain to "reconcile" the second and third tiers of the Taliban so that the West can finally quit this fight and allow the Afghans to work out their future on their own terms.

Conciliation of this sort is not true "reconciliation," and it certainly will not lead to Justice. The flaw in such an approach is to pretend that outreach to "reconcilable" elements among the Taliban and other local networks is really some form of healing of relationships. If there is to be conciliation, it will not be due to a moral epiphany among the Taliban or tribal leaders nor to appeals to justice and brotherhood. Any arrangement that brings the Taliban in "from the cold" must be based on a reappraisal of their interests. That appraisal might be based on major military victories that leave the Taliban and its tribal allies stricken and on the verge of collapse, allowing its members to switch sides. A reframing of the Taliban's, and tribal, interests might include the opportunity for it to participate in governance, such as an evolution to being a political party. We have seen elsewhere how rebel groups can disband and become part of the political process, as occurred with Colombia's M-19 in 1991 and Iraq's Sunni Awakening in 2007. That "reframing" of interests could take place in the context of culturally relevant mechanisms of arbitration (*sulh*) and/or a formal Afghan loya jirga.

Any such agreement would begin with assessments about security and political order from both sides. On the U.S./NATO side, the calculation would have everything to do with a cost/benefit analysis of the national security implications of exiting Afghanistan.[13] Moreover, the West will have to come to terms with the failure of an economic development-first strategy: the West still mistakenly thinks economic development is the root of Order when, in truth, it is the fruit of stability and security. For the Taliban, such a political bargain would proceed from a definition of their interests over the short and long term on the larger stage of Afghan national politics. In short, we should not confuse the lingo of "Afghan reconciliation" with the reconciliatory ideals found in Western conflict resolution theory; Afghan political "reconciliation"—if it is to happen—will be about Order and interests, not harmony and healing.

## Conclusion

This book would be a success if a lieutenant in Kandahar, an aid worker in South Sudan, a diplomat in Sri Lanka, and a student at Oxford could hold up three fingers and say, "Order, Justice, Conciliation . . . that is the goal!" None of these individuals would have to expound upon the history of the just war tradition, nor would they have to know in detail all the elements of the 200-page Army Stabilization Manual or the State Department's 53-page "Post-Conflict Reconstruction Essential Tasks" list. They need not be experts in the full range of post-conflict strategies across disciplines, but they should be expert in their narrow field and understand how their efforts contribute to Order, Justice, and/or Conciliation. Furthermore, their leaders should have keen appreciation for the imperative of Order, its relationship to Justice, and the possibilities of Conciliation in national policy.

In order to achieve this "success," a new generation of just war scholarship is needed, one that actively engages the hard jus ad bellum and jus in bello cases facing the world: transnational terrorism, piracy, robotics, UAVs and drones, cyber warfare, and weapons of mass effect. This scholarship must also take into account the changing political landscape offered by post–Cold War innovations in international law and the emergence of supranational institutions like the EU and UN. In addition to all of this, there is critical need for prudential, principled scholarship on war's end, especially the application of the Order-Justice-Conciliation framework to specific cases as well as work furthering the linkages to conflict resolution, transitional justice, and other fields as introduced in chapter six. War is unlikely to go away for good, but by ending some wars well we will constrain one of the principal causes of future wars.

# Afterword

This manuscript was largely completed in 2010. Thus, just before it goes to press (spring 2012), it is worth reflecting briefly on the many political developments of the past two years, particularly in the cases discussed herein. Of course, in most instances little has changed: East Timor and the Balkans remain tense, with outsiders footing tremendous bills for peace and security. The size and poverty of some of these places make it hard to imagine that they will ever be robust, thriving countries. Pakistan is more violent and less stable today. On the other side of the border, President Obama's "surge" of troops (which is consonant with this book's emphasis on Order) was complemented by a 2011 "peace jirga," led by former President Rabbani. However, as foreshadowed in chapter 7, Rabbani was assassinated and the reconciliation process derailed, at least for a time. In Iraq, as of March 2012, the government is largely on its own after the last Coalition forces departed at the end of 2011. Not surprisingly, a variety of non-state actors immediately stepped up violent attacks to disrupt political order and stability, and the country is almost paralyzed politically as (Shiite) Prime Minister Maliki attempts to imprison (Sunni) Vice President Tariq al-Hashemi, who has fled to sanctuary in the Kurdish north.

However, in other cases small steps at progress continue to be made. In contrast to most people's expectations—mine included—South Sudan broke away in a mostly peaceful secession decided by popular referendum. There has been North versus South and Northerner versus Southerner violence, but deaths have been in the hundreds rather than the hundreds of thousands. However, South Sudan is another runt-state, like East Timor and Kosovo: small, weak, drastically underdeveloped and impoverished, and in many ways at the mercy of the goodwill and interests of its neighbors and the international community.

Interestingly, Rwanda just won a long-standing extradition case in Canada to bring one of the Hutu radicals back to Kigali for Rwandan, not UN (ICTR), justice. This individual famously called the Tutsis "cockroaches" worthy of elimination. Perhaps justice will finally be served. Not far from Rwanda, the African Union has finally decided to act robustly in anarchic Somalia because of the destabilizing effects of terrorism, migration, and poverty in the region. However, the wider uncertainty induced by the Arab Spring, including the implosion of regimes in Egypt, Syria, and Yemen, creates tremendous anxiety regarding disorder across the entire Near East. Most of us in the West are cheering efforts for democracy, human rights, and the rule of law in that region, but I am deeply concerned about the erosion of political order there.

I have argued throughout this book that "ending wars well" takes hard work, coordination, investment, and modesty. In January 2012 the United States announced significant cuts to its conventional military forces, suggesting far fewer overseas interventions in the near future. This parallels a dramatic cut in European defense spending due to the European economic crisis. Without Western leadership, it is unclear that other rising powers, such as China, will invest manpower and materiel toward orderly post-conflict transitions. On a positive note, the U.S. State Department has incrementally increased its post-conflict resources over the past four years, elevating its "office" for coordinating reconstruction and stabilization assistance to the level of "bureau" for "conflict and stabilization operations," led by an assistant secretary of state. These types of signals are important when it comes to planning and resource allocation.

Finally, 2012's most dramatic development was the revolution, aided by NATO and allied airstrikes, which toppled the autocracy of Muammar Gadhafi. In the Libyan case, the outside world is trying desperately to help the Libyans achieve Order lest society disintegrate into a real civil war along regional and tribal cleavages. Much of the old regime was quickly swept away by the swift justice of the 2011 revolution. This book suggests that the transitional government of Libya (not to mention new governments in Juba, Cairo, and Tunis as well as potentially new governments at some point in Sana'a, Mogadishu, Damascus, and elsewhere) must devote its attention and modest resources first to founding a durable, secure Order in politics, the economy, and at the borders, then thoughtfully consider whether any further efforts at national Justice are necessary and thus reconcile all Libyans to a shared future.

# Notes

## CHAPTER 1. ENDING WARS WELL

1. "Rumsfeld: No World War III in Iraq," published November 15, 2002, http://archives.cnn.com/2002/US/11/15/rumsfeld.iraq/index.html. Accessed August 10, 2009.

2. Ivo Daalder, *Pew Case Studies in International Affairs #462: The Clinton Administration and Multilateral Peace Operations* (Washington DC: Georgetown University Institute for the Study of Diplomacy Publications, 1994): 4.

3. David Kilcullen, *The Accidental Guerrilla* (Oxford: Oxford University Press, 2009), 121–22.

4. A vast literature has developed on this point. For three different perspectives, see Bob Woodward, *Plan of Attack* (New York: Simon and Schuster, 2004); Douglas Feith, *War and Decision* (San Francisco: Harper-Collins, 2005); Nora Berensahl, *After Saddam: Pre-War Planning and the Occupation of Iraq* (Santa Monica, CA: RAND, 2008).

5. Thomas Hobbes, *Leviathan*, ed. Edwin Curley (Indianapolis, IN: Hackett, 1994): chapter 13, par. 8.

6. Samuel P. Huntington, *Political Order in Changing Societies* (New York: Columbia University Press, 1968).

7. The reader will note the influence of Reinhold Niebuhr, *The Irony of American History* (New York: Scribners, 1952) on this paragraph.

8. Ken Booth, *Theory of World Security* (New York: Cambridge University Press, 2007).

9. Eric Patterson and Kendra Puryear, "Outlaws and Barbarians: The Bush Administration's Revolution in Sovereignty," *The Whitehead Journal of Diplomacy and International Relations* 7(1) (Winter-Spring 2006): 199–211.

10. Martin Cook makes this point well, particularly with regards to the R2P documents. See his "Accountability for Intervention/Protection Activities," Paper presented at the Workshop on Ethics of Intervention/Protection, John Jay College of Criminal Justice, New York, January 2010.

11. James Turner Johnson, *Morality and Contemporary Warfare* (New Haven, CT: Yale University Press, 1999), 34.

12. "Just War—or a Just War?" published March 9, 2003. http://www.nytimes.com/2003/03/09/opinion/just-war-or-a-just-war.html?pagewanted=1. Accessed September 29, 2010.

13. "Iraq an unjust war, Walzer argues," published October 5, 2006. http://www.dailyprincetonian.com/2006/10/05/16073/. Accessed September 29, 2010.

14. William Galston, comments made at the Pew Forum's "Iraq and Just War: A Symposium," September 30, 2002. http://pewforum.org/Politics-and-Elections/Iraq-and-Just-War-A-Symposium.aspx. Accessed September 29, 2010.

15. President Barack Obama, Nobel Peace Prize Acceptance Speech, Oslo, Norway, December 10, 2009. http://www.msnbc.msn.com/id/34360743/. Accessed September 22, 2010.

16. John McCain, "Why We Must Win," *Washington Post*, August 31, 2003, Editorial: B07.

17. "Asymmetric Warfare & Just War," published February 10, 2003. http://article.nationalreview.com/267923/asymmetrical-warfare-just-war/michael-novak. Accessed September 29, 2010.

18. "Fighting a Just War in Iraq," published April 8, 2003. http://www.heritage.org/Research/Reports/2003/04/Fighting-a-Just-War-in-Iraq. Accessed September 29, 2010.

19. "List of Operations," http://www.un.org/en/peacekeeping/list.shtml. Accessed September 29, 2010.

CHAPTER 2.
NEW JUST WAR THINKING ON POST-CONFLICT

1. President Barack Obama, Nobel Peace Prize Acceptance Speech, Oslo, Norway, December 10, 2009. For the full transcript see: http://www.msnbc.msn.com/id/34360743/ (last accessed September 22, 2010).

2. There are some works that make comparison of these schools their primary aim. For instance, Richard B. Miller, *Interpretation of Conflict: Ethics, Pacifism, and the Just-War Tradition* (Chicago: University of Chicago Press, 1991). A brief summary is made in J. Darryl Charles, *Between Pacifism and Jihad: The Christian and the Just War* (Colorado Springs, CO: Intervarsity Press, 2005).

3. A slightly different approach is applied by A. J. Coates, who contrasts four "images of war": pacifism, just war, militarism, and realism. See his *The Ethics of War* (Manchester: Manchester University Press, 1997).

4. See Samuel P. Huntington, "The Clash of Civilizations?" *Foreign Affairs* 72(3) (Summer 1993): 22–49.

5. For a description of these phenomena, see Mark Juergensmeyer, *Terror in the Mind of God* (Berkeley: University of California Press, 2003).

6. Helen Ellerbe, *The Dark Side of Christian History* (San Rafael, CA: Morningstar Books, 1995), p. 74.

7. President Barack Obama, Nobel Peace Prize Acceptance Speech, Oslo, Norway, December 10, 2009.

8. Charles reports on the historical context and position of early church fathers such as Tertullian (who thought that political and military service were forms of pagan sacrifice) and Origen—both of whom admit that Christians were serving in the Roman military. J. Daryl Charles, "Presumption against War or Presumption against Injustice? The Just War Tradition Reconsidered," in *Journal of Church and State* 48(3) (Fall 2005). Charles points out that even the Quaker pacifist Roland Bainton suggests that the occupation of soldiering was likely not completely off limits to early Christians in Bainton's *Christian Attitudes Toward War and Peace* (New York: Abingdon, 1960), 66, 81.

A somewhat one-sided view of the historic Christian pacifist position is Geoffrey Nuttall, *Christian Pacifism in History* (Berkeley, CA: World Without War Council, 1971). For a thoughtful look at historical and contemporary Christian pacifism from its most famous contemporary defender, see John Howard Yoder, *The Original Revolution: Essays on Christian Pacifism*, Christian Peace Shelf Series (Philadelphia: Herald Press, 2003). A history of the application of pacifism in American politics is Theron F. Schlabach et al., *Proclaim Peace: Christian Pacifism from Unexpected Quarters* (Urbana: University of Illinois Press, 1997).

9. Frederick H. Russell discusses how the limited teaching of Christ on violence ultimately resulted in early Church leaders, such as Origen and later Ambrose and Augustine, having to define a Christian position on military service, allegiance to the state, and war in general. See his *The Just War in the Middle Ages* (Cambridge: Cambridge University Press, 1975), chap. 2.

10. John Langan, S.J., takes a slightly different approach to varieties of pacifism. He distinguishes those withdrawn from the controversy surrounding a given war from those who take an activist and ideological or politicized pacifist stance. "Just War Theory After the Gulf War," in *Theological Studies* 53 (1992): 99–100.

11. See Niebuhr's "An Open Letter to Richard Roberts," *Christianity and Society* 5 (Summer 1940). This argument is updated in thoughtful chapters by Paul Ramsey, William V. O'Brien, and Jean Bethke Elshtain in their edited volume *Just War Theory* (New York: New York University Press, 1992).

12. Sometimes Costa Rica is held up as such an example: it abolished its military in 1948. Costa Rica, however, has robust national "police" forces and, like every other country, it is not immune to threats within and without its territory.

In the summer of 2010, Costa Rica began to host a large U.S. military presence to fight the rapidly expanding militias of transnational drug syndicates.

13. The dedication of the document reads, "In commemoration of the tenth anniversary of the bishops' pastoral letter, *The Challenge of Peace: God's Promise and Our Response*, and the thirtieth anniversary of Pope John XXIII's encyclical letter, *Pacem in Terris*, an ad hoc subcommittee of the Committee on International Policy drafted and approved a statement on peacemaking in a post–Cold War world. This statement, *The Harvest of Justice Is Sown in Peace*, was approved by the NCCB Administrative Board in September 1993, was submitted to and approved by the full body of bishops on November 17, 1993 and is authorized for publication as a reflection of the National Conference of Catholic Bishops by the undersigned. . ." (Washington, D.C.: U.S.C.C., 1983). The document can be found at http://www.nccbuscc.org/sdwp/harvest.htm (accessed January 1, 2007).

14. The former area is often the domain of philosophers, such as John Lango's "The Just War Principle of Last Resort: The Question of Reasonableness Standards," *Asteriskos: Journal of International and Peace Studies* 1 (2006): 1–2 and his "Generalizing and Temporalizing Just War Principles: Illustrated by the Principle of Just Cause," in *Rethinking the Just War Tradition*, ed. M. Brough, J. W. Lango, and H. van der Linden (Albany: State University of New York Press, 2007). The ethics of decisions to go to war continues to be argued on a case-by-case basis, such as in Jean Bethke Elshtain's *Just War Against Terror* (New York: Basic Books, 2004); Eric Patterson's *Just War Thinking War* (Lanham, MD: Lexington Books, 2007); John Lango's "Is There a Just Cause for Current U.S. Military Operations in Afghanistan?" *International Journal of Applied Philosophy* 24(1) (2010); see Ignatieff's *The Lesser Evil: Political Ethics in an Age of Terror* (Princeton: Princeton University Press, 2004); Joseph McMillan's monograph *Apocalyptic Terrorism: The Case for Preventive Action*, Institute for National Strategic Studies (November 2004); Jonathan I. Charney, "The Use of Force against Terrorism and International Law," in *American Journal of International Law* 95(4) (October 2001). Of course, for the classic modern looks at issues of WMDs and total war, see Paul Ramsey, *The Just War: Force and Political Responsibility*, rev. ed. (Lanham, MD: Rowman and Littlefield, 2002), and Michael Walzer, *Just and Unjust Wars*, 3d ed. (New York: Basic Books, 2000). A contrasting view is Henry Shue, "Liberalism: The Impossibility of Justifying Weapons of Mass Destruction," in *Ethics and Weapons of Mass Destruction: Religious and Secular Perspectives*, ed. Sohail H. Hashmi and Steven P. Lee (Cambridge: Cambridge University Press, 2004).

15. The "presumption against force school" is associated with James F. Childress. See his "Just-War Theories" in *Theological Studies* 39 (1978) and "Just-War Criteria" in *War or Peace? The Search for New Answers*, ed. Thomas A. Shannon (Maryknoll, NY: Orbis Books, 1980), as well as the Catholic Bishops' letter *The Challenge of Peace* (1986) and its successor *The Harvest of Justice* (1993).

This revisionist view has been thoughtfully rebuked in many quarters, most notably by James Turner Johnson's *Morality and Contemporary Warfare* (New Haven, CT: Yale University Press, 1999) and his "Just War, As It Was and Is" in *First Things* 149 (January 2005). Also see J. Daryl Charles, "Presumption against War or Presumption against Injustice? The Just War Tradition Reconsidered," in *Journal of Church and State* 48(3) (Fall 2005). Richard B. Miller defends the position of the Catholic bishops based on the notion of prima facie duties in "Aquinas and the Presumption Against Killing and War," *Journal of Religion* 82(2) (April 2002).

16. Kjell-Ake Nordquist, *From 'Just War' to Justified Intervention* (Uppsala: Department of Theology Publications, 1998); Dean K. Chatterjee and Don E. Scheid, *Ethics and Foreign Intervention* (Cambridge: Cambridge University Press, 2003); Robert L. Philips and Duane L. Cady, *Humanitarian Intervention: Just War vs. Pacifism* (Lanham, MD: Rowman and Littlefield, 1996); Terry Nardin, "The Moral Basis of Humanitarian Intervention" in *Ethics and International Affairs* 14(1) (2002); Nicholas J. Wheeler's *Saving Strangers: Humanitarian Intervention in International Society* (New York: Oxford University Press, 2001).

17. A contemporary example focused on ethics but without a just war foundation on asymmetric tactics from torture to heat rays, is Michael Gross's *The Moral Dilemmas of War* (Cambridge: Cambridge University Press, 2010).

18. James Turner Johnson, "Maintaining the Protection of Non-Combatants," *Journal of Peace Research* 37(4) (July, 2000); Eric Patterson and Teresa Casale, "Targeted Killing and the War on Terror" in *International Journal of Intelligence and Counterintelligence* 18(4) (Winter 2005); Mikael F. Nabati, "Anticipatory Self-Defense: The Terrorism Exception," *Current History* (May 2003); preventive and preemptive action is explored by Eric A. Posner and Alan O. Sykes, in "Optimal War and *Jus ad Bellum*," University of Chicago Law & Economics, Olin Working Paper No. 211/University of Chicago, Public Law Working Paper No. 63 (April 2004). Available at: http://ssrn.com/abstract=546104 (Accessed September 15, 2005). An earlier work, considering issues surrounding the decisions on intervention in the first Gulf War, is Ramsey, O'Brien, and Elshtain, eds., *Just War Theory*.

19. Many of the authors in Patterson and Gallagher elucidate these controversies, most notably James Turner Johnson's essay "Debates over Just War and Jihad: Ideas, Interpretations, and Implications Across Cultures" in Eric Patterson and John P. Gallagher, eds., *Debating the War of Ideas* (New York: Palgrave-Macmillan, 2009). Pauletta Otis, "More than a War of Ideas: Ideology, Theology and Religion," in *Ideas as Weapons: Influence and Perception in Modern Warfare*, ed. G. J. David, Jr. and T. McKeldin III (Sterling, VA: Potomac Press, November 2008). Also see John Kelsay, *Arguing Just War in Islam* (Cambridge, MA: Harvard University Press, 2007).

20. David B. Rivkin, Jr., Lee A. Casey, and Darin R. Bartram, "Bringing Al-Qaeda to Justice: The Constitutionality of Trying Al-Qaeda Terrorists in the

Military Justice System," Legal Memorandum #3, Policy Research and Analysis Series, Heritage Foundation, available at http://www.heritage.org/Research/ LegalIssues/LM3.cfm (accessed May 30, 2005); Noah Feldman, "Choices of Law, Choices of War" in *Harvard Journal of Law and Public Policy* 25(2) (Spring 2002); Adam Roberts, "Transformative Military Occupation: Applying the Laws of War and Human Rights," *American Journal of International Law* 100 (July 2006): 618–22.

21. A thoughtful article that argues for human rights and justice but recognizes the limitations of the international system is Geoffrey Best's "Justice, International Relations, and Human Rights," the 21st Martin Wight Memorial Lecture, London School of Economics and Political Science (9 March 1995), printed in *International Affairs* 71(4). Chris Brown's argument regarding the limitations of international justice remains relevant today; see his "Theories of International Justice" in *British Journal of Political Science* 27(2) (April, 1997). An argument from justice is Peter Temes, *The Just War: An American Reflection on Morality in Our Time* (New York: Ivan R. Dees, 2004). Adam Roberts, "Transformative Military Occupation: Applying the Laws of War and Human Rights," *American Journal of International Law* 100 (July 2006); Brian Orend, *War and International Justice* (Ontario, Canada: Wilfred Laurier University, 2000). A critic of the "rights-based" approach to just war thinking is Oliver O'Donovan. See his insightful short book, *The Just War Revisited* (Cambridge: Cambridge University Press, 2003).

22. A thoughtful article applying traditional just war criteria to economic sanctions in the case of Haiti is Albert G. Pierce's "Just War Principles and Economic Sanctions" in *Ethics and International Affairs* 10 (1996). Other pieces on sanctions using a slightly different approach to justice are Joy Gordon's "A Peaceful, Silent, Deadly Remedy: The Ethics of Economic Sanctions," in *Ethics and International Affairs* 13 (1999); and Thomas G. Weiss's "Sanctions as a Foreign Policy Tool: Weighing Humanitarian Impulses," in *Journal of Peace Research* 36(5) (September 1999). A recent application to the world of spies is Angela Gendron, "Just War, Just Intelligence: An Ethical Framework for Foreign Espionage," in *International Journal of Intelligence and Counterintelligence* 18 (Fall, 2005).

23. An ecological application is Gregory Reichberg and Henrik Syse's "Protecting the Natural Environment in Wartime: Ethical Considerations from the Just War Tradition," in *Journal of Peace Research* 37(4) (July 2000).

24. Paul Ramsey, *The Just War: Force and Political Responsibility*, rev. ed. (Lanham, MD: Rowman and Littlefield, 2002) and *War and the Christian Conscience: How Shall Modern War Be Conducted Justly?* (Durham, NC: Duke University Press, 1961, 1985); Michael Walzer, *Just and Unjust Wars*, 3d ed. (New York: Basic Books, 2000); Jean Bethke Elshtain, *Just War Against Terror* (New York: Basic Books, 2003).

25. Walzer, *Just and Unjust Wars.*

26. Walzer, *Arguing About War* (New Haven: Yale University Press, 2004), 163.

27. See James Turner Johnson, *Morality and Contemporary Warfare* (New Haven, CT: Yale University Press, 1999), 142.

28. Gary J. Bass, "Jus Post Bellum," *Philosophy and Public Affairs* 32(4) (Fall 2004): 384–413.

29. Dan Caldwell and Robert E. Williams, Jr., *Seeking Security in an Insecure World* (Oxford: Rowman & Littlefield, 2006).

30. Doug McCready, "Ending the War Right: Jus Post Bellum and the Just War Tradition," *Journal of Military Ethics*, 8(1) (March 2009), 66–78.

31. Davida E. Kellogg, "Jus Post Bellum: The Importance of War Crimes Trials," *Parameters* 32 (2002): 87–99.

32. Camilla Bosanquet, "Refining Jus Post Bellum," Paper for the annual meeting of the International Society for Military Ethics (formerly JSCOPE), (January 25–26, 2007).

33. Louis V. Iasiello, "Jus in Bello: Key issues for a contemporary assessment of just behavior in war" (January 1, 2003). Doctoral dissertation at Salve Regina University.

34. Mark Evans, "Moral Responsibilities and Conflicting Demands of Jus Post Bellum," *Ethics and International Affairs* 23(2) (2009): 159.

## CHAPTER 3.
## THE PRIMACY OF ORDER

1. http://www.cnn.com/2003/WORLD/meast/05/01/sprj.irq.main/.

2. http://www.globalsecurity.org/wmd/library/news/iraq/2003/05/iraq-030523-rfel-081430.htm.

3. Aristotle, *Politics*, trans. Benjamin Jowett (Chicago: University of Chicago Press, 1984); Augustine, *The City of God*, ed. David Knowles (New York: Penguin Classics, 1984); Thomas Hobbes, *Leviathan*, ed. Richard Tuck (New York: Penguin Classics, 1982); Hugo Grotius, *The Rights of War and Peace*, ed. Richard Tuck (Oxford: Oxford University Press, 2001); Samuel P. Huntington, *Political Order in Changing Societies*.

4. *Politics* I: 1253a31–3.

5. See Jean Bethke Elshtain, *Augustine and the Limits of Politics* (South Bend, IN: University of Notre Dame Press, 1993).

6. Roger Epp, "The Augustinian Moment in International Politics," International Politics Research Papers, No. 10 (Aberystwyth, U.K.: Department of International Politics, University College of Wales, 1991).

7. Thomas Hobbes, *Leviathan*, ed. Edwin Curley (Indianapolis, IN: Hackett, 1994), chapter 13, par. 9.

8. Ibid, chapter 13, par. 1.

9. Ibid.

10. Tim Judah, *Kosovo: War and Revenge*, 2nd ed. (New Haven, CT: Yale University Press, 2002).

11. The Albanian polity essentially collapsed due to ubiquitous Ponzi scheme failures in early 1997, resulting in widespread looting and the loss of public order—including the dismembering of government armories. For more, see Alex Cost, "A Preventable Tragedy: Warning Signs about Albania Had Been There for All to See," in *The Gazette* (March 21, 1997).

12. See Wes Johnson, *Balkan Inferno: Betrayal, War and Intervention 1990–2005* (New York: Enigma Books, 2007), esp. chap 4.

13. These details are available in the Executive Summary to the U.S. Department of State's report on Kosovo, "Ethnic Cleansing in Kosovo: An Accounting; December 1999," available at: http://www.state.gov/www/global/ human_rights/kosovoii/homepage.html.

14. Peter Beaumont, "Kosovo breakaway from Serbia was legal, world court rules" in *The Guardian* (July 22, 2010). Available at: http://www.guardian.co.uk/ world/2010/jul/22/kosovo-breakaway-serbia-legal-world-court.

15. Such details are available at the NATO website. See http://www.nato.int/ issues/kfor/index.html. Accessed August 20, 2008.

16. This data is listed on the MONUC UN website. See http://www.un.org/ depts/dpko/missions/monuc/facts.html. Accessed August 20, 2008.

17. See the UN website for details http://www.un.org/Depts/dpko/missions/ unmiset/facts.html.

18. Such details are available at both the NATO and ISAF websites. See http://www.nato.int/issues/afghanistan/040628-factsheet.htm. Accessed June 18, 2008.

19. See the UN report on lessons learned in Somalia http://www.un.org/ Depts/dpko/lessons/UNOSOM.pdf. Accessed August 21, 2008.

20. According to the UN, as of April 30, 2010, there were 16,883 troops, 253 military observers, and 4,797 police officers plus an additional 4,000 civilians working in Darfur under UN auspices. The latest approved budget (2009–2010) was for $1.5 billion, and this is separate from other specific national contributions such as USAID's $127.6 million for refugees. Little of this funding and personnel is directed at decisive action toward an enduring political order.

21. See the UN report on least developed countries http://www.un.org/ special-rep/ohrlls/ldc/list.htm. Accessed August 21, 2008.

22. See the Voice of America report on aid for Kosovo http://www.voanews. com/uspolicy/2008-07-18-voa5.cfm. Accessed August 21, 2008.

23. See the UN report on UNMEE http://www.un.org/Depts/dpko/ missions/unmee/facts.html. Accessed August 21, 2008.

24. Introduction to the executive summary of the Comprehensive Proposal for the Kosovo Status Settlement, also known as the Ahtissari Plan, available at http://www.unosek.org/unosek/en/statusproposal.html.

25. To review the full Comprehensive proposal for Kosovo Status Settlement, see http://www.unosek.org/unosek/en/statusproposal.html.

26. See the UN basic fact sheet on UNMIK. http://www.unmikonline.org/docs/2008/Fact%20Sheet%20July%202008.pdf. Accessed August 21, 2008.

27. Of course, there are two other places where such investment has occurred: Afghanistan and Iraq. However, neither of these cases is a parallel example of true international humanitarian intervention of traditional peacekeeping. Both were directly attacked by conventional Western military forces, and true to America's post-war model, both received massive security and humanitarian assistance to rebuild, modernize, and democratize in ways most similar to the destruction and absolute surrender of Japan and Germany and subsequent rebuilding by the Allied Powers.

28. For additional information on this controversy, see the BBC's reporting: http://news.bbc.co.uk/2/hi/africa/1559624.stm and http://news.bbc.co.uk/2/hi/africa/161445.stm.

29. See BBC's reporting: http://news.bbc.co.uk/2/hi/africa/232803.stm.

30. See ICG, *Sudan: Preventing Implosion*, International Crisis Group, Africa Briefing No. 68 (17 December 2009), accessed July 21, 2010, available at http://www.crisisgroup.org/.

31. For a complete breakdown of FY 2010 spending, please see http://www.usaid.gov/locations/sub-saharan_africa/countries/sudan/docs/jun10_monthly_update.pdf. For a complete breakdown of USAID spending in Sudan, please see http://www.usaid.gov/locations/sub-saharan_africa/sudan/monthly_archive.html.

32. Preliminary Statement of The Carter Center Election Observation Mission in Sudan Presidential, Gubernatorial, and Legislative Elections, April 17, 2010. Available at: http://www.cartercenter.org/news/pr/sudan-041710.html.

33. See K. Almquist, Renewed Conflict in Sudan, Contingency Planning Memorandum No. 7, Center for Preventive Action, Council on Foreign Relations (March 2010), accessed July 21, 2010, available at http://www.cfr.org/publication/21678/renewed_conflict_in_sudan.html.

CHAPTER 4.
JUSTICE

1. See David Cordingly, *The Billy Ruffian: The Bellerophon and the Downfall of Napoleon* (New York: Bloomsbury USA, 2003); Philip Dwyer, *The French Revolution and Napoleon: A Sourcebook* (London: Routledge, 2002); Alan Schom, *One Hundred Days: Napoleon's Road to Waterloo* (San Francisco: Harper-Collins, 1998).

2. Daniel J. Philpott, unpublished manuscript, "Just and Unjust Peace: An Ethic of Political Reconciliation," p. 13.

3. Brian Orend, *War and International Justice* (Ontario: Wilfred Laurier University Press, 2000), 227.

4. Nigel Biggar, "Making Peace or Doing Justice: Must We Choose?" and Jean Bethke Elshtain, "Politics and Forgiveness," in *Burying the Past: Making*

*Peace and Doing Justice After Civil Conflict*, ed. Nigel Biggar (Washington D.C.: Georgetown University Press, 2003). Mohamed Othman, "Justice and Reconciliation," and Howard Adelman, "Rule-Based Reconciliation," in *Roads to Reconciliation*, ed. Elin Skaar et al. (Lanham, MD: Lexington Books, 2005).

5. Elshtain, "Politics and Forgiveness."

6. Western discussions of reparations usually occur in the context of twentieth-century Allied victories in the World Wars. One rarely reads scholarship on "reparations" demanded by a victorious aggressor against its victims. Again, the notion of restitution needs conceptual clarity.

7. There is a long list of references on this topic, one of the most interesting being Robert E. Bunselmeyer, *Cost of the War 1914–1919: British Economic War Aims and the Origins of Reparation* (London: Archon, 1975). For a post-hoc (revised) look at his country's own policies, see David Lloyd George, *Truth About Reparations and War Debts* (London: Howard Fertig, 1970).

8. Critics of the use of sanctions as a blunt tool for punishment include T. Clifton Morgan and Valerie L. Schwebach, "Fools Suffer Gladly: The Use of Economic Sanctions in International Crises." *International Studies Quarterly* 41(1) (March, 1997), and Kim Richard Nossal, "International Sanctions as International Punishment," *International Organization* 43(2) (Spring, 1998).

9. "US Pays Millions to Civilian Victims of Collateral Damage," published December 20, 2005, http://www.spacewar.com/reports/US_Pays_Millions_To_ Civilian_Victims_Of_Collateral_Damage.html. Accessed September 29, 2010; "U.S. Pays Up for Fatal Iraq Blunders," published November 26, 2003, http://www.twf.org/News/Y2003/1126-Claims.html. Accessed September 29, 2010; http://www.twf.org/News/Y2003/1126-Claims.html.

10. For an extensive discussion, see Eric Patterson, *Just War Thinking*, (Lanham, MD: Lexington Books, 2007), chap. 5.

11. Orend, *War and International Justice*, 227.

12. Jason McClure, "Hague Court Rules on Damages in Ethiopia-Eritrea War," published August 18, 2009, http://www.bloomberg.com/apps/news?pid=2 0601116&sid=aBQPEvKH8kzo. Accessed August 22, 2009.

13. O'Donovan, *The Just War Revisited*, 55. He is citing Francisco de Vitoria, *Political Writings*, edited and translated by Anthony Pagden and Jeremy Lawrence (Cambridge and New York: Cambridge University Press, 1991), 327.

14. GAO/NSIAD-91-160 Persian Gulf Relief Effort. The Government Accountability Office. 13 April 1991. P. 4. Accessed 30 September 2010 http://archive.gao.gov/d21t9/143444.pdf.

15. "Resolution 687 (1991)," April 3, 1991, http://daccess-dds-ny.un.org/doc/RESOLUTION/GEN/NR0/596/23/IMG/NR059623.pdf?OpenElement. Accessed September 29, 2010.

16. "Iraq still owes Kuwait 22.3 bln in reparations from Gulf war," published August 17, 2010, http://www.worldbulletin.net/news_detail.php?id=62672. Accessed September 29, 2010.

17. "The Coalition Provisional Authority," last modified July 6, 2007, http://www.iraqcoalition.org/. Accessed September 29, 2010.

18. "Iraq Economic Data (1989–2003)," last modified April 23, 2007, https://www.cia.gov/library/reports/general-reports-1/iraq_wmd_2004/chap2_annxD.html. Accessed September 29, 2010.

19. "IRAQ: The Regime's Debt," published December 31, 2003, http://www.cfr.org/publication/7796/iraq.html. Accessed September 29, 2010.

20. "Resolution 1483 (2003)," published May 22, 2003, http://www.loc.gov/law/help/hussein/docs/SC%20Res%201483%202003.pdf. Accessed September 29, 2010.

21. "Saddam Hussein Trial," posted July 3, 2007, http://www.loc.gov/law/help/hussein/index.php. Accessed August 20, 2009.

22. Technically, the umbrella political organization for Tutsis was the Rwandan Patriotic Front (RPF). Although the army associated with it is, to be precise, the Rwanda Patriotic Army (RPA), for the purpose of this summary and to follow common usage, the terms will be collapsed into RPF.

23. "Frontline: Rwanda Chronology," http://www.pbs.org/wgbh/pages/frontline/shows/rwanda/etc/cron.html. Accessed August 28, 2004.

24. Ibid.

25. Samantha Power, *A Problem from Hell: America and the Age of Genocide* (New York: Perennial, 2002), 353.

26. Gerard Prunier, *The Rwanda Crisis 1959–1994: History of a Genocide* (New York: Columbia University Press, 1995), 282.

27. This summary of the Rwandan genocide is largely drawn from the following sources: Gerald Caplan, *Rwanda: The Preventable Genocide,* The Report of the International Panel of Eminent Personalities to Investigate the 1994 Genocide in Rwanda and the Surrounding Events (Organization of African Unity, 1998); Gilbert M. Khadiagala, "The Case of Rwanda" (Paper prepared for the National Intelligence Council Project on Intervention in Internal Conflict, December, 2001); Power, *A Problem from Hell*; Prunier, *The Rwanda Crisis*; Helen M. Hintjens, "Explaining the 1994 Genocide in Rwanda." *Journal of Modern African Studies* 37(2) (1999): 241–286; Stephen Kinzer, *A Thousand Hills: Rwanda's Rebirth and the Man Who Dreamed It* (Hoboken, N.J.: John Wiley & Sons, 2008); Wm. Cyrus Reed, "Exile, Reform, and the Rise of the Rwandan Patriotic Front," *Journal of Modern African Studies* 34(3) (1996): 479–501; Josias Semujanga, *Origins of Rwandan Genocide* (New York: Humanity Books, 2003); Richard Vokes, "The Arusha Tribunal: Whose Justice?" *Anthropology Today* 18(5) (2002); Barbara Walter, "The Critical Barrier to Civil War Settlement," *International Organization* 51(3) (1997): 335–364.

28. For a comprehensive discussion of these issues, see Olivier Dubois, "Rwanda's National Criminal Courts and the International Tribunal," *International Review of the Red Cross* 321 (December 31, 1997): 717–731.

29. S/PV.3453, p. 15. Ambassador Bakuramutsa stated that Rwanda still believed that the international community's interest in creating the tribunal was a face-saving measure since it had not reacted to save Rwanda from the genocide even though it was present locally. See "1945–1995: Critical Perspectives of the Nuremberg Trials and State Accountability," Fifth Ernst C. Stieffel Symposium, *New York Law School Journal of Human Rights,* 12 (1995), 650.

30. "ORGANIC LAW No. 08/96 of August 30,1996 on the Organization of Prosecutions for Offences constituting the Crime of Genocide or Crimes against Humanity committed since October 1, 1990," last modified December 5, 2000, http://www.preventgenocide.org/law/domestic/rwanda.htm. Accessed September 29, 2010.

31. Rwanda's Organic Law can be found in its entirety at the following internet address. These categories are taken directly from the site. "ORGANIC LAW No. 08/96 of August 30,1996 on the Organization of Prosecutions for Offences constituting the Crime of Genocide or Crimes against Humanity committed since October 1, 1990," last modified December 5, 2000, http://www.preventgenocide.org/law/domestic/rwanda.htm. Accessed September 29, 2010.

32. Ibid.

33. Human Rights Watch 2004, p.18 – From December 1996 to December 2006, the courts managed to try about 10,000 suspects.

34. "Rwanda's Grass Roots," published July 10, 2004, http://www.nytimes. com/2004/07/10/opinion/rwanda-s-grass-courts.html?scp=1&sq=Rwanda+gaca ca+courts&st=nyt. Accessed September 29, 2010. *New York Times Online,* July 10, 2004.

35. *BBC News,* March 10, 2005.

36. "Gacaca Closure Now Scheduled For June 30," published April 12, 2010, http://www.hirondellenews.com/content/view/13360/332/. Accessed September 29, 2010.

37. Indeed, the chaotic security environment contributed to a decade of war in the eastern portion of neighboring Democratic Republic of Congo, which has left an estimated five million dead.

38. Chapter VII, Article 49 of the UN Charter.

39. These cases include trials completed and awaiting verdict, cases where the closing arguments have yet to be heard, ongoing trials, new trials, and one re-trial. These data and other facts about the Tribunal are available from the Tribunal's website (www.ictr.org) and are listed specifically in the Letter dated 14 May 2009 from the President of the International Criminal Tribunal for Rwanda addressed to the president of the Security Council (S/2009/247).

40. Judge Dennis Byron, Address to the United Nations Security Council, "Six Monthly Report on the Completion Strategy: the International Criminal Tribunal for Rwanda," 4 June 2009. Available at www.ictr.org/ENGLISH/ speeches/byron090604.htm.

41. See "How Rwanda's traditional courts are speeding up trials of genocide suspects" at NewsfromAfrica.com, 13 June 2009, Zachary Ochieng. Available at http://www.newsfromafrica.org/newsfromafrica/articles/art_11624.html.

42. The fourth case is based in the Central African Republic, but the perpetrators are alleged to have committed crimes in Eastern DRC.

43. Filip Reyntjens and Stef Vandeginste, "Rwanda: An Atypical Transition," *Roads to Reconciliation,* ed. Elin Skaar et al. (Lanham, MD: Lexington Books, 2005), 100.

44. Ibid., 102.

45. Ibid.

## CHAPTER 5.
## CONCILIATION

1. Al Nofi, comp. "Statistics on the War's Costs." Louisiana State University. http://web.archive.org/web/20070711050249/http://www.cwc.lsu.edu/other/stats/warcost.htm. Accessed September 13, 2010.

2. Jay Winik, *April 1865: The Month That Saved America* (New York: HarperCollins, 2001).

3. James McPherson, *Battle Cry of Freedom* (Oxford: Oxford University Press, 1988). Maris Vinovskis, *Toward a Social History of the American Civil War: Exploratory Essays* (Cambridge: Cambridge University Press, 1990).

4. Jean Bethke Elshtain, "Politics and Forgiveness," in *Burying the Past,* 51.

5. Ibid., 53.

6. David A. Crocker, "Truth Commissions, Transitional Justice, and Civil Society," in *Truth vs. Justice: The Morality of Truth Commissions,* ed. Robert I. Rotberg et al. (Princeton: Princeton University Press, 2000).

7. Kenneth Waltz, *Man, the State, and War* (New York: Columbia University Press, 1954).

8. Clive Archer and Pertti Joenniemi, *The Nordic Peace* (Hampshire, U.K.: Ashgate, 2003).

9. There is a growing literature on domestic reconciliation, forgiveness, and intra-state change. For examples see A. Boraine et al., *Dealing with the Past: Truth and Reconciliation in South Africa* (Cape Town: IDASA, 1994); Brian Frost, *The Politics of Peace* (London: Darton, Longman, and Todd, 1991); James L. Gibson and Amanda Gouws, "Truth and Reconciliation in South Africa: Attributions of Blame and the Struggle over Apartheid," *American Political Science Review* 93(3) (September, 1999); Neil J. Kritz, ed., *Transitional Justice: How Emerging Democracies Reckon with Former Regimes,* vol. 2 (Washington, DC: US Institute of Peace, 1995); Dan Markel, "The Justice of Amnesty? Towards a Theory of Retributivism in Recovering States," *University of Toronto Law Journal* 49(3) (Summer, 1999); Martha Minow, *Between Vengeance and Forgiveness* (Boston: Beacon Press, 1998); Andrew Rigby, *Justice and Reconciliation* (Boulder, CO: Lynne

Rienner, 2001); "Accommodating Individual Criminal Responsibility and National Reconciliation: The UN Truth Commission for East Timor," *American Journal of International Law* 95(4) (October, 2001); Barbara F. Walter, "The Critical Barrier to Civil War Settlement," *International Organization* 51(3) (Summer, 1997).

10. Immanuel Kant, *Perpetual Peace and Other Essays*, trans. T. Humphrey (Indianapolis, IN: Hackett, 1983); Jean Jacques Rousseau, *"The Social Contract" and Other Later Political Writings*, ed. Victor Gourevitch (Cambridge: Cambridge University Press, 1997).

11. Patterson, *Just War Thinking*, chap. 5.

12. William J. Long and Peter Brecke, "War and Reconciliation," *International Interactions* 25(2) (July 1999): 95–117. This point is important because the traditional definition of war is 1,000 battle deaths; Long and Brecke's definition of conflict as including only 32 deaths per year widely extends their possible cases beyond traditional wars to other forms of political violence and transition.

13. Willy Brandt's efforts at reconciliation with Poland and the Soviet Union bore fruit in the form of treaties bringing closure to issues outstanding since 1945. Those treaties were signed a quarter-century after the war's end, in 1970. Likewise, the Egypto-Israeli "Camp David Accords" were signed in 1978—a full generation after the birth of Israel and successive Arab-Israeli wars in 1948, 1956, 1967, and 1973. So too, many of the other cases indicate many years between the end of an international conflict and the start of political conciliation: 7 years between the end of World War II and Japan's public conciliation with countries it had attacked (such as China, India, France, and Australia among others); 26 years between the end of the Sino-Indian war and a reconciliation event in 1988; 22 years between the end of the Vietnam war and public reconciliation in 1995; a decade between the end of the Ethiopia-Somalia conflict and a modest conciliatory event. In all of these cases, the international environment had profoundly changed, often one or more regimes had changed, and the strategic context of national interests made modest efforts at conciliation possible. Few of these cases had the drama of Sadat or Brandt, but all were evidence of changes in government-to-government relations.

14. "Person of the Year: Anwar Sadat," published January 2, 1978, http://www.time.com/time/subscriber/personoftheyear/archive/stories/1977.html. Accessed September 29, 2010.

15. Ibid.

16. Ibid.

17. "President Anwar Sadat's Address to the Israeli Knesset," given November 20, 1977, http://www.ibiblio.org/sullivan/docs/Knesset-speech.html. Accessed September 29, 2010.

18. A UN report documenting the period of Indonesian rule records approximately 180,000 civilian deaths during this time, including many from a

deliberate starvation policy. See "UN Verdict on East Timor," *The Australian,* published January 19, 2006, www.yale.edu/gsp/east_timor/unverdict/html. Accessed March 16, 2009. For a more detailed history, see James Dunn's *Timor: A People Betrayed* (Sydney: ABC Books, 1996).

19. The UN and other documents can be found at East Timor's Commission for Reception, Truth, and Reconciliation (http://www.cavr-timorleste.org/) and Yale University's East Timor Project (http://www.yale.edu/gsp/east_timor/).

20. Michael J. Kelly et al., "Legal Aspects of Australia's Involvement in the International Force for East Timor," *International Review of the Red Cross,* no. 841 (March 31, 2001): 101–139. Available at http://www.icrc.org/eng/resources/documents/misc/57jqz2.htm.

21. See Report of the International Commission of Inquiry on East Timor to the Secretary-General, UN Doc. A/54/726-S/2000/59.

22. James Cotton, "Australia's East Timor Experience: Military Lessons and Security Dilemmas." Available at http://www.nids.go.jp/english/event/symposium/pdf/2002/sympo_e2002_10.pdf.

23. Jarat Chopra, "The UN's Kingdom of East Timor," in *Survival* 42(27) (2000), and Carsten Stahn, "The UN Transitional Administrations in Kosovo and East Timor: A First Analysis" (2001) Max Planck Y.B. UN L. 105.

24. Dionisio Babo-Soares, "Nahe Biti: Grassroots Reconciliation in East Timor," in Elin Skaar, Siri Gloppen, and Astri Suhrke, eds., *Roads to Reconciliation* (Lanham, MD: Lexington Books, 2003), 225.

25. Ibid., 238.

26. Carsten Stahn, "Accommodating Individual Criminal Responsibility and National Reconciliation: The UN Truth Commission for East Timor," *American Journal of International Law* 95(4) (October 2001): 952–66.

27. Human Rights Watch backgrounder "Justice Denied for East Timor." Available at www.hrw.org/legacy/backgrounder/asia/timor/etimor1202bg.htm. Accessed March 16, 2009.

28. Stahn, "Accommodating Individual Criminal Responsibility and National Reconciliation: The UN Truth Commission for East Timor."

29. Ibid.


CHAPTER 6.
CONNECTIONS AND CONTRADICTIONS

1. Giovanni Sartori, "Concept Misinformation in Comparative Politics," *American Political Science Review* 64(4) (December, 1970): 1033–1053.

2. Minow, *Between Vengeance and Forgiveness,* 9.

3. These essays have been compiled into a single, massive compendium entitled *Turbulent Peace: The Challenges of Managing International Conflict,* Chester A. Crocker et al. (Washington, D.C.: U.S. Institute of Peace, 2001). The

discussion about democracy and post-conflict includes chapters 44–46, Pauline H. Baker, "Conflict Resolution versus Democratic Governance: Divergent Paths to Peace?" Roland Paris, "Wilson's Ghost: The Faulty Assumptions of Post-Conflict Peacebuilding," and Timothy D. Sisk, "Democratization and Peacebuilding: Perils and Promises."

4. John Paul Lederach, "Just Peace: The Challenge of the 21st Century." Available from the European Platform for Conflict Prevention and Transformation, http://www.gppac.net/documents/pbp/part1/1_justpe.htm. Accessed September 29, 2010.

5. Barbara F. Walter, "Designing Transitions from Civil War: Demobilization, Democratization, and Commitments to Peace," *International Security* 24(1) (Summer, 1999): 137.

6. Rama Mani, *Beyond Retribution: Seeking Justice in the Shadows of War* (Malden, MA: Blackwell, 2001).

7. "Mozambique: Religious Peacebuilders Broker End to Civil War," The Berkley Center for Religion, Peace & World Affairs. http://repository.berkleycenter.georgetown.edu/010210MozambiqueCaseStudy.pdf. Accessed September 29, 2010.

8. Samuel P. Huntington, *The Third Wave: Democratization in the Late Twentieth Century* (Oklahoma City: University of Oklahoma Press, 1993).

9. Guillermo O'Donnell, *Modernization and Bureaucratic-Authoritarianism: Studies in South American Politics* (Berkeley: University of California, 1963); Adam Prezerworski and Henry Teune, eds., *Democracy and Local Governance: Ten Empirical Studies* (Honolulu: Matsunaga Institute, 1994).

10. For an introduction to many such truth commissions, see Priscilla B. Hayner, "Fifteen Truth Commissions—1974 to 1994: A Comparative Study," *Human Rights Quarterly* 16(4) (Spring 1994).

11. "The Universal Declaration of Human Rights," adopted and proclaimed on December 10, 1948. http://www.un.org/en/documents/udhr/index.shtml. Accessed September 29, 2010.

12. A survey of the humanitarian literature found only a handful of significant citations of the just war tradition. One of the very few to reference just war is Kjell Erling Kjellman in an article focused on what she calls "injustice frames": tools for promoting new norms in international life (in this case activism against landmines and cluster munitions). The article is not about just war, but the author does observe, "Discrimination, for instance, is one of the oldest notions of the just doctrine of war, contending that civilians are not to be the intentional objects of attack during conflict." More common is the positivist approach that seems blithely unaware that the just war tradition provides the overall basis for the laws of armed conflict. For example, Don Hubert seems not to know that the just war tradition even exists, as he locates the history of proportionality within

the past century. He rightly observes that proportionality as a concept was helpful for the International Committee of the Red Cross to argue from due to its historical and legal punch. However, amazingly, and wrongly, the author writes, "The principle of proportionality emerged through the 1868 St. Petersburg Declaration on Explosive Projectiles and the 1899 and 1907 Hague Conventions on Expanding Bullets and War on Land, respectively. The principle of discrimination originated with the 1907 Hague Convention on War on Land and was reflected in the 1949 Geneva Convention on the Protection of Civilian Persons in Time of War," quoted in "The Landmine Ban: A Case Study in Humanitarian Advocacy," Providence: Institute for International Studies, 2000. This is stunning in its short-term, positivist understanding of where these principles came from, with the entire paper making absolutely no reference to the historic just war tradition.

13. This is the HALO Trust. Don Hubert, "The Landmine Ban: A Case Study," Thomas J. Watson Jr. Institute for International Studies: Occasional Paper 42 (2000): xii.

14. "Quick Impact, Quick Collapse: the Danger of Militarized Aid in Afghanistan," http://www.oxfam.org/policy/quick-impact-quick-collapse. Accessed September 29, 2010.

15. Marion Harroff-Tavel, "Does It Still Make Sense to Be Neutral?" in *Humanitarian Exchange* (December 2003). Available at: http://www.odihpn.org/documents%5Chumanitarianexchange025.pdf

16. Neil Narang, "Exploring the Impact of Humanitarian Aid in Conflict and Post-Conflict Areas," Paper presented at the annual meeting of the International Studies Association, February 17, 2010, in New Orleans.

17. Walzer, *Arguing About War*, 14.

18. "Convention on the Prohibition of the Use, Stockpiling, Production and Transfer of Anti-Personnel Mines and on Their Destruction," adopted and proclaimed on September 18, 1997. http://www.un.org/Depts/mine/UNDocs/ban_trty.htm. Accessed September 29, 2010.

19. Eric Patterson, *Just War Thinking*, chap. 5.

20. LTC Albert Marin, Assistant Chief of Staff of the Plans and Operations Division, U.S. Forces, Korea, and CPT Litzelman, Civil Affairs and Psychological Operations Officer with Special Operations Command, Korea, "Peacemakers Along the DMZ: Non-Self Destruct Landmines in the Republic of Korea," *Journal of Mine Action* 6(1) (April 2002).

## CHAPTER 7.
## 21ST-CENTURY CHALLENGES

1. The video of this presentation is available at: http://berkleycenter. georgetown.edu/events/the-aftermath-of-war-reflections-on-jus-post-bellum. Accessed March 15, 2011.

2. The International Commission on Intervention and State Sovereignty, "The Responsibility to Protect" (2004), 42.

3. Ibid., 43.

4. The United Kingdom has developed an interagency hub for dealing with "stabilization operations" involving the Ministry of Defence, the Foreign and Commonwealth Office, and the Department for International Development (DFID).

5. *Post-Conflict Reconstruction Essential Tasks,* Office of the Coordinator for Reconstruction and Stabilization, U.S. Department of State (April 2005) (54 pages). This document, in tandem with the *Whole of Government Reconstruction and Stabilization (R&S) Planning and Execution Process* document (2008, 85 pages), provides guidance on how-to.

6. DoD Instruction 3000.05, "Stability Operations," was first issued in 2005; it was reissued in 2009. The updated version can be found at http://www.dtic.mil/whs/directives/corres/pdf/300005p.pdf. Accessed September 30, 2010.

7. The USAID toolkit series is designed for classroom use with practitioners. It can be found at http://www.usaid.gov/our_work/cross-cutting_ programs/conflict/publications/toolkits.html. Accessed September 30, 2010.

8. See Army FM 3-07, "Stability Operations," chapter 2 (2.6).

9. See UNDP's Afghan New Beginnings website, http://www.undpanbp. org. A second phase of DDR began with Presidential Decree 50 in the summer of 2004. This declared any extant militias to be "illegally armed groups" and essentially was a final chance for such individuals and their leaders to demobilize. With the advent of national assembly elections the next year and concerns about Afghan security, a second formal program called Disarmament of Illegally Armed Groups (DIAG) began. The "carrot" was that the leaders of illegally armed groups (regional and local militias) could participate in the elections if their groups disarmed; the "stick" was that those who had not/would not disband their fighting forces were barred from office. DIAG was largely unsuccessful except in a few cases.

10. Combatants who demobilized participated in a formal ceremony, often with a military parade or review, handed in a weapon (often an antique model inferior to what they kept hidden), attended a seminar, and received compensation consisting primarily of food and clothing. The former militia members, after two decades of war, were to return to their families and become productive citizens.

International Center for Transitional Justice (ICTJ), "Disarmament and Transitional Justice in Afghanistan" (2008). Available at http://www.ictj.org/en/ research/projects/ddr/country-cases/2376.html.

11. See AIHRC's website at http://www.aihrc.org.af. See ICTJ, p. 3.

12. Eric Patterson and John P. Gallagher, *Debating the War of Ideas* (New York: Palgrave-Macmillan, 2009).

13. Another issue is at stake. The U.S., unlike a traditional imperial power, has a critical normative dilemma: American values infuse notions of what a systematic justice must look like. Unlike the colonizer who allows the local headman to handle affairs of public order and morality as he sees fit (as long as the rubber, gold, or ivory keeps coming), the U.S. has a normative commitment to justice. This is not a matter of just courts, clerks, notaries, etc. but, more basically, the principles of impartiality, fairness, equity, the rule of law, etc. What the United States cannot settle for is a country that institutionalizes the violation of essential human rights. In short, the principal U.S. ethical challenge with regard to justice is balancing its strategic interests, including withdrawing troops, with the most fundamental value commitments, chiefly human rights, basic civil liberties, and the rule of law.

# Index